THE
MEDITERRANEAN
COOKBOOK

The Mediterranean Cookbook

13-Digit ISBN: 978-1-64643-049-9
10-Digit ISBN: 1-64643-049-2

This book may be ordered by mail from the publisher. Please include $5.99 for postage and handling. Please support your local bookseller first!

Books published by Cider Mill Press Book Publishers are available at special discounts for bulk purchases in the United States by corporations, institutions, and other organizations. For more information, please contact the publisher.

Cider Mill Press Book Publishers
"Where good books are ready for press"
501 Nelson Place
Nashville, Tennessee 37214

cidermillpress.com

Typography: Adobe Garamond Pro, Black Jack, Gotham, Type Embellishments One

Image Credits: Photos on pages 15, 41, 59, 71, 72, 79, 100, 103, 104, 107, 108, 111, 112, 115, 117, 118, 121, 124, 130, 133, 137, 138, 141, 142, 145, 146, 149, 153, 154, 158, 162, 182, 204, 207, 208, 211, 212, and 216 courtesy of Cider Mill Press Book Publishers.
Photo on page 239 © StockFood / Einenkel, Udo. Photo on page 240 © StockFood / Westermann & Buroh Studios.
Photo on page 243 © StockFood / Grablewski, Alexandra. Photo on page 244 © StockFood / Gräfe & Unzer Verlag / Walter, Axel.
All other images used under official license from Shutterstock.com.

Printed in China

Back cover image:
Moussaka, see page 180.

Front endpaper image:
Skillet Salmon, see page 223.

Back endpaper image:
Lamb & Cannellini Soup, see page 113.

23 24 25 26 27 DSC 8 7 6 5 4

THE
MEDITERRANEAN
COOKBOOK

A Regional Celebration of Seasonal, Healthy Eating

CIDER MILL
PRESS

BOOK
PUBLISHERS

TABLE *of* CONTENTS

INTRODUCTION

It seems obvious that any region spanning places as distinctive as Morocco, the Peloponnese, Catalonia, and the South of France would struggle to find much common ground.

And while the cultures that occupy these spots are in themselves unique and fascinating, the rest of the world has come to lump them together for two reasons (other than the obvious one—their proximity to the celebrated sea): the general health and longevity enjoyed by their residents, and the diet that produces this salubrious state.

At a time when a number of other developed countries are having considerable issues with obesity and chronic, diet-related diseases, more and more people have started to gravitate to the region—at least in terms of the choices they make when deciding what they are going to consume.

This means a focus on seafood, vegetables, fruits, nuts, and whole grains, a move away from the poultry, eggs, and dairy most modern diets center upon, sporadic-at-most encounters with red meat, and a strict avoidance of the refined oils and processed foods that contribute to many of the health issues that have cropped up in the contemporary world.

These guidelines are then inflected by the various seasoning-and-vegetable preferences of each culture that dwells within the region, giving rise to a unique, rich, and varied diet that provides a nearly endless amount of options, flavors, and dishes to choose from, helping practitioners of the Mediterranean diet avoid the monotony that sinks so many other efforts to improve one's health through the food that they eat.

Diet is not enough, of course—regular exercise and quality rest are other key factors in improving one's fitness. But it might be argued that the biggest advantage of the Mediterranean diet is how easy both of these become when one is fueled by the lighter food and more balanced meals that it encourages.

It would be a mistake to confuse lighter with less flavorful (and it's pretty easy to see that this assumption leads to most of the mistakes people make in terms of their food choices). While a desire to retain the fresh taste of the excellent ingredients available in the area is foremost, there are still plenty of delightful moments packed in these pages, making it easy for all to prioritize their health, and enjoy their nightly excursion around the region.

CHAPTER 1

SNACKS

---

*Going Mediterranean means that your diet will become
focused in a completely different direction than what you're used to.
When this shift is combined with its emphasis on lightness, many
assume that there is positively no room for snacking.*

*That's not necessarily the case, as the recipes in this chapter show.
All delicious and able to provide the benefits that have brought this style of
eating to the fore, you can comfortably turn to this section anytime
you're in need of something to tide you over till dinner, or are
looking for treats that can proudly fill out a platter.*

YIELD: **4 SERVINGS**

ACTIVE TIME: **5 MINUTES**

TOTAL TIME: **10 MINUTES**

Honeyed Figs

INGREDIENTS

6 TABLESPOONS HONEY

16 BLACK MISSION FIGS, HALVED

½ TEASPOON CINNAMON

GOAT CHEESE, CRUMBLED,
TO TASTE

DIRECTIONS

1. Place the honey in a nonstick skillet and warm over medium heat.

2. When the honey starts to liquefy, place the figs in the skillet, cut side down, and cook until they start to brown, about 5 minutes.

3. Sprinkle the cinnamon over the figs and gently stir to coat. Remove the figs from the pan, top with the goat cheese, and serve.

YIELD: **4 SERVINGS**

ACTIVE TIME: **15 MINUTES**

TOTAL TIME: **24 HOURS**

Spicy Chickpeas

INGREDIENTS

1 CUP DRIED CHICKPEAS, SOAKED OVERNIGHT AND DRAINED

2 CUPS VEGETABLE OIL

1 TEASPOON SMOKED PAPRIKA

½ TEASPOON ONION POWDER

½ TEASPOON BROWN SUGAR

¼ TEASPOON GARLIC POWDER

¼ TEASPOON KOSHER SALT

PINCH OF CHILI POWDER

DIRECTIONS

1. Bring water to a boil in a saucepan. Add the chickpeas, reduce heat so that the water simmers, and cook until the chickpeas are tender, about 40 minutes. Drain the chickpeas, place them on a paper towel–lined plate, and pat them dry.

2. Place the oil in a Dutch oven and warm it to 350°F over medium heat.

3. Place the remaining ingredients in a bowl, stir until thoroughly combined, and set the mixture aside.

4. Place the chickpeas in the hot oil and fry until golden brown, about 3 minutes. Remove and place them in the bowl with the seasoning mixture. Toss to coat and serve.

Stuffed Peppadew Peppers

INGREDIENTS

1 (14 OZ.) JAR OF
PEPPADEW PEPPERS

½ LB. FETA OR GOAT CHEESE

¼ CUP OLIVE OIL

¼ CUP FINELY CHOPPED
FRESH BASIL

DIRECTIONS

1. Drain the peppadew peppers, but don't rinse them. Carefully stuff the cheese into the peppers' cavities, taking care not to tear the delicate peppers, and place them on a plate.

2. Drizzle olive oil over the stuffed peppers and sprinkle the basil on top.

Lahmacun

YIELD: **1 FLATBREAD**

ACTIVE TIME: **10 MINUTES**

TOTAL TIME: **30 MINUTES**

INGREDIENTS

1 BALL OF PIZZA DOUGH

3 TABLESPOONS LAHMACUN SPREAD (SEE SIDEBAR)

JUICE OF 1 LEMON WEDGE

SUMAC POWDER, TO TASTE

¼ SMALL RED ONION, SLICED

3 SLICES OF TOMATO

¼ CUCUMBER, PEELED AND JULIENNED

1 TABLESPOON CRUMBLED FETA CHEESE

OLIVE OIL, TO TASTE

FRESH MINT LEAVES, FOR GARNISH

DIRECTIONS

1. Preheat the oven to 410°F and place a baking stone in the oven as it warms. Place the dough on a piece of parchment paper and gently stretch it into a very thin round. Cover the dough with the Lahmacun Spread.

2. Using a peel or a flat baking sheet, transfer the dough to the heated baking stone in the oven. Bake for about 10 minutes, until the crust is golden brown and starting to char. Remove and top with the lemon juice, sumac powder, onion, tomato, cucumber, and feta. Drizzle olive oil over the top and garnish with fresh mint leaves.

LAHMACUN SPREAD

Place ¾ lb. ground beef, ½ large onion, chopped, ½ green bell pepper, 1 chopped tomato, 1 bunch of fresh parsley, 1½ teaspoons tahini, 1 tablespoon tomato paste, ¼ teaspoon of red pepper flakes, black pepper, and ground nutmeg, ½ teaspoon of cinnamon, allspice, sumac powder, dried thyme, and table salt, and the juice of 1 lemon wedge in a food processor or blender and puree until the mixture is a smooth paste.

YIELD: **1 FLATBREAD**

ACTIVE TIME: **10 MINUTES**

TOTAL TIME: **30 MINUTES**

Za'atar Manaqish

INGREDIENTS

1 BALL OF PIZZA DOUGH

2 TABLESPOONS ZA'ATAR
SEASONING

2 TABLESPOONS OLIVE OIL

¼ SMALL RED ONION, SLICED

3 SLICES OF TOMATO

¼ CUCUMBER, PEELED
AND JULIENNED

2 TABLESPOONS CRUMBLED
FETA CHEESE

1 HANDFUL OF GREEN
OLIVES, PITTED

DIRECTIONS

1. Preheat the oven to 400°F and place a baking stone in the oven as it warms. Place the dough on a piece of parchment paper and gently stretch it into a very thin round. Spread the za'atar and olive oil over the dough.

2. Using a peel or a flat baking sheet, transfer the dough to the heated baking stone in the oven. Bake for about 10 minutes, until the crust is golden brown and starting to char. Remove and top with the onion, tomato, cucumber, feta, and olives.

Minty Pickled Cucumbers

INGREDIENTS

½ CUP SUGAR

½ CUP WATER

½ CUP RICE VINEGAR

2 TABLESPOONS DRIED MINT

1 TABLESPOON CORIANDER SEEDS

1 TABLESPOON MUSTARD SEEDS

2 CUCUMBERS, SLICED

DIRECTIONS

1. Place all of the ingredients, except for the cucumbers, in a small saucepan and bring to a boil, stirring to dissolve the sugar.

2. Place the cucumbers in a large mason jar. Remove the pan from heat and pour the brine over the cucumbers. Let cool completely before using or storing in the refrigerator, where the pickles will keep for 1 week.

YIELD: **4 SERVINGS**

ACTIVE TIME: **5 MINUTES**

TOTAL TIME: **15 MINUTES**

Kale Chips

INGREDIENTS

1 BUNCH OF KALE,
STEMS REMOVED

1 TEASPOON KOSHER SALT

½ TEASPOON PEPPER

½ TEASPOON PAPRIKA

½ TEASPOON DRIED PARSLEY

½ TEASPOON DRIED BASIL

¼ TEASPOON DRIED THYME

¼ TEASPOON DRIED SAGE

2 TABLESPOONS OLIVE OIL

DIRECTIONS

1. Preheat the oven to 400°F. Tear the kale leaves into smaller pieces and place them in a mixing bowl. Add the remaining ingredients and work the mixture with your hands until the kale pieces are evenly coated.

2. Divide the seasoned kale between 2 parchment-lined baking sheets so that it sits on each in an even layer. Place in the oven and bake until crispy, 6 to 8 minutes. Remove and let cool before serving.

Roasted Artichoke & Garlic Spread

YIELD: **1 CUP**

ACTIVE TIME: **5 MINUTES**

TOTAL TIME: **15 MINUTES**

INGREDIENTS

¾ LB. ARTICHOKE HEARTS, QUARTERED

4 GARLIC CLOVES

2 TABLESPOONS APPLE CIDER VINEGAR

¼ TEASPOON KOSHER SALT

¼ CUP OLIVE OIL

PINCH OF ONION POWDER (OPTIONAL)

DIRECTIONS

1. Preheat the oven's broiler to high. Place the artichoke hearts on a baking sheet and broil, turning them occasionally, until browned all over, about 10 minutes.

2. Place the artichoke hearts in a food processor, add the remaining ingredients, and blitz until the desired texture for the spread is achieved.

Sweet Potato & Tahini Dip with Spiced Honey

YIELD: **1 CUP**

ACTIVE TIME: **15 MINUTES**

TOTAL TIME: **1 HOUR**

INGREDIENTS

1 SWEET POTATO, HALVED

OLIVE OIL, AS NEEDED

1 YELLOW ONION, QUARTERED

2 LARGE GARLIC CLOVES, UNPEELED

¼ CUP TAHINI DRESSING (SEE PAGE 35)

1 TEASPOON FRESH LEMON JUICE

½ TEASPOON KOSHER SALT

2 TABLESPOONS HONEY

½ TEASPOON ANCHO CHILI POWDER

1 TABLESPOON MINCED PISTACHIOS, FOR GARNISH

DIRECTIONS

1. Preheat the oven to 400°F. Place the sweet potato, cut side down, and the onion on an oiled baking sheet. Place the garlic cloves in a small piece of aluminum foil, place a few drops of oil on them, wrap them up, and place on the baking sheet.

2. Place the baking sheet in the oven and roast for approximately 20 minutes, then remove the garlic. Roast the sweet potato and onion for another 10 minutes, or until the potato is very tender. Remove from the oven and let cool.

3. Scoop the sweet potato's flesh into a food processor. Add the roasted onion, peeled garlic cloves, Tahini Dressing, lemon juice, and salt. Pulse until the mixture is a smooth paste. Taste and adjust seasoning as necessary.

4. Place the honey in a very small saucepan and warm it over low heat. Add the ancho chili powder, remove the pan from heat, and let sit for a few minutes to infuse the honey.

5. Place the puree in a shallow bowl and make a well in the center. Pour some of spiced honey in the well and garnish with the pistachios.

YIELD: **4 SERVINGS**

ACTIVE TIME: **20 MINUTES**

TOTAL TIME: **30 MINUTES**

Zucchini Rolls

INGREDIENTS

3 SMALL ZUCCHINI, SLICED INTO
¼-INCH-LONG SLICES

2 TABLESPOONS OLIVE OIL

SALT AND PEPPER, TO TASTE

3 TABLESPOONS GOAT CHEESE

1 TABLESPOON CHOPPED
FRESH PARSLEY

½ TEASPOON FRESH LEMON JUICE

2 OZ. BABY SPINACH,
FINELY CHOPPED

3 TABLESPOONS PINE NUTS

FRESH BASIL, FINELY CHOPPED,
TO TASTE

DIRECTIONS

1. Preheat your gas or charcoal grill to medium heat (400°F). Brush the zucchini slices with the olive oil and season them with salt and pepper.

2. Place the zucchini on the grill and cook until charred on both sides and tender, about 8 minutes.

3. Place the goat cheese, parsley, and lemon juice in a bowl and stir to combine.

4. Spread the goat cheese mixture over the grilled zucchini. Sprinkle the spinach, pine nuts, and basil over the spread and then roll the slices up. Secure the rolls with toothpicks and serve.

YIELD: **16 PITAS**

ACTIVE TIME: **1 HOUR**

TOTAL TIME: **3 HOURS AND 30 MINUTES**

Pita Bread

INGREDIENTS

2¼ TEASPOONS ACTIVE DRY YEAST

2½ CUPS LUKEWARM WATER (90°F)

3 CUPS ALL-PURPOSE FLOUR,
PLUS MORE AS NEEDED

2 TABLESPOONS OLIVE OIL

1 TABLESPOON KOSHER SALT

3 CUPS WHOLE WHEAT FLOUR

BUTTER, AS NEEDED

DIRECTIONS

1. Place the yeast and the water in a bowl and gently stir. Let the mixture sit until it starts to foam, about 10 minutes.

2. Place the yeast mixture in a large mixing bowl. Add the all-purpose flour and stir until a stiff dough forms. Cover the bowl with plastic wrap and let the dough rise for about 1 hour.

3. Add 1 tablespoon of the oil and the salt to the dough and knead to incorporate. Incorporate the whole wheat flour in ½-cup increments and then stir until the dough is soft. Place the dough on a flour-dusted work surface and knead until it is smooth and elastic, about 10 minutes.

4. Oil a large mixing bowl with butter. Place the ball of dough in the bowl, cover it loosely with plastic wrap, place in a naturally warm spot, and let it rise until doubled in size, about 45 minutes to 1 hour.

5. Place the dough on a flour-dusted work surface, punch it down, and cut it into 16 pieces. Place the pieces on a baking sheet and cover with a damp kitchen towel while working with individual pieces. Roll out the pieces until they are approximately 7 inches in diameter. Stack the pita, placing sheets of plastic wrap between each one.

6. Warm a cast-iron skillet over high heat and add the remaining olive oil. Working with one pita at a time, cook for about 20 seconds on one side, then flip and cook for a minute on the other side, until bubbles form. Turn over again and cook until the pita puffs up, another minute or so. Store the cooked pitas under a kitchen towel until ready to serve.

Baba Ganoush

INGREDIENTS

2 EGGPLANTS

2 GARLIC CLOVES, CHOPPED

¼ CUP TAHINI DRESSING
(SEE PAGE 35)

½ TEASPOON FRESH LEMON JUICE

1 TEASPOON KOSHER SALT

½ TEASPOON CUMIN

½ TEASPOON PAPRIKA

¼ TEASPOON CAYENNE PEPPER

2 TABLESPOONS OLIVE OIL

1 TABLESPOON FINELY CHOPPED
FRESH PARSLEY, FOR GARNISH

DIRECTIONS

1. Preheat the oven to 400°F. Pierce the skin of the eggplants with a knife or fork and place them on a baking sheet. Place them in the oven and roast for about 35 minutes, until the skin is blistered and the flesh is tender. Remove from the oven and let cool.

2. Peel the eggplants and chop the flesh. Place it in a bowl with the remaining ingredients, except for the parsley, and stir to combine. Garnish with the parsley and serve.

TIP: For a creamier texture, use a food processor to puree the eggplants before incorporating the rest of the ingredients.

Tahini Dressing

INGREDIENTS

½ HEAD OF GARLIC

6 TABLESPOONS FRESH
LEMON JUICE

1 TEASPOON KOSHER SALT

1 CUP TAHINI

½ TEASPOON CUMIN

ICE WATER, AS NEEDED

DIRECTIONS

1. Place the unpeeled garlic cloves and the lemon juice in a blender. Add a pinch of the salt and blitz until the mixture is a coarse puree. Let the mixture stand for 10 minutes.

2. Working over a large mixing bowl, strain the puree through a fine sieve and press down on the solids to extract as much liquid as possible. Discard the solids and add the tahini, cumin, and remaining salt to the mixing bowl. Whisk until smooth and creamy, adding water as needed if the mixture needs thinning out. Use immediately or store in the refrigerator for up to 1 week.

YIELD: **4 SERVINGS**

ACTIVE TIME: **10 MINUTES**

TOTAL TIME: **1 HOUR AND 10 MINUTES**

Herbed Goat Cheese

INGREDIENTS

½ LB. GOAT CHEESE

2 TABLESPOONS FINELY CHOPPED FRESH TARRAGON

2 TABLESPOONS FINELY CHOPPED FRESH CHIVES

2 TABLESPOONS FINELY CHOPPED FRESH THYME

1 CUP OLIVE OIL

DIRECTIONS

1. Slice the goat cheese into thick rounds. Gently roll the rounds in the herbs and gently press down so that they adhere to the surface of the cheese.

2. Layer the rounds in glass jars. Pour the olive oil over them until they are covered. Let the mixture sit for an hour before serving.

NOTE: The herbs listed here are simply suggestions. Feel free to use any herb or spice you like.

YIELD: **2 CUPS**

ACTIVE TIME: **5 MINUTES**

TOTAL TIME: **5 MINUTES**

Olive Tapenade

INGREDIENTS

1½ CUPS CURED BLACK OR KALAMATA OLIVES, PITTED

1 TEASPOON WHITE MISO PASTE

3 TABLESPOONS CAPERS, RINSED

1½ TABLESPOONS FINELY CHOPPED FRESH PARSLEY

3 GARLIC CLOVES

3 TABLESPOONS FRESH LEMON JUICE

¼ TEASPOON BLACK PEPPER, PLUS MORE TO TASTE

¼ CUP OLIVE OIL

SALT, TO TASTE

DIRECTIONS

1. Place the olives, miso paste, capers, parsley, garlic, lemon juice, and black pepper in a food processor and pulse until coarsely chopped.

2. Drizzle the olive oil into the mixture and pulse a few more times until a chunky paste forms, scraping down the work bowl as needed. Season with salt and pepper and serve.

YIELD: **6 SERVINGS**

ACTIVE TIME: **45 MINUTES**

TOTAL TIME: **1 HOUR AND 15 MINUTES**

Tiropitakia

INGREDIENTS

½ LB. FETA CHEESE

1 CUP GRATED KEFALOTYRI
CHEESE

¼ CUP FINELY CHOPPED
FRESH PARSLEY

2 EGGS, BEATEN

BLACK PEPPER, TO TASTE

1 (1 LB.) PACKAGE OF FROZEN
PHYLLO DOUGH, THAWED

2 STICKS OF UNSALTED
BUTTER, MELTED

DIRECTIONS

1. Place the feta cheese in a mixing bowl and break it up with a fork. Add the kefalotyri, parsley, eggs, and pepper and stir to combine. Set the mixture aside.

2. Place 1 sheet of the phyllo dough on a large sheet of parchment paper. Gently brush the sheet with some of the melted butter, place another sheet on top, and brush this with more of the butter. Cut the phyllo dough into 2-inch strips, place 1 teaspoon of the filling at the end of the strip closest to you, and fold over one corner to make a triangle. Fold the strip up until the filling is completely covered. Repeat with the remaining sheets of phyllo dough and filling.

3. Preheat the oven to 350°F and oil a baking sheet with some of the melted butter. Place the pastries on the baking sheet and bake in the oven until golden brown, about 15 minutes. Remove and let cool briefly before serving.

YIELD: **2 CUPS**

ACTIVE TIME: **5 MINUTES**

TOTAL TIME: **1 HOUR AND 5 MINUTES**

Tzatziki

INGREDIENTS

1 CUP PLAIN FULL-FAT YOGURT

¾ CUP SEEDED AND MINCED CUCUMBER

1 GARLIC CLOVE, MINCED

JUICE FROM 1 LEMON WEDGE

SALT AND WHITE PEPPER, TO TASTE

FRESH PARSLEY OR DILL, FINELY CHOPPED, TO TASTE

DIRECTIONS

1. Place the yogurt, cucumber, garlic, and lemon juice in a mixing bowl and stir to combine. Taste and add salt and pepper as needed. Stir in the parsley or dill.

2. Place in the refrigerator and chill for 1 hour before serving.

White Bean & Rosemary Spread

YIELD: **2 CUPS**

ACTIVE TIME: **5 MINUTES**

TOTAL TIME: **35 MINUTES**

INGREDIENTS

1 (14 OZ.) CAN OF CANNELLINI BEANS, DRAINED AND RINSED

2 TABLESPOONS OLIVE OIL

2 TEASPOONS BALSAMIC VINEGAR

2 GARLIC CLOVES, MINCED

1 TABLESPOON FINELY CHOPPED FRESH ROSEMARY

½ CELERY STALK, MINCED

SALT AND PEPPER, TO TASTE

2 PINCHES OF RED PEPPER FLAKES

DIRECTIONS

1. Place half of the beans in a bowl and mash them. Add the rest of the beans, the olive oil, vinegar, garlic, rosemary, and celery and stir to combine.

2. Season with salt, pepper, and red pepper flakes and cover the bowl with plastic wrap. Refrigerate for about 30 minutes before serving.

LEMON-PEPPER MAYONNAISE

Place 1 cup mayonnaise, 3 tablespoons grated Parmesan cheese, 1 tablespoon lemon zest, 3 tablespoons fresh lemon juice, 1½ teaspoons black pepper, and 2 teaspoons kosher salt in a mixing bowl and whisk until combined.

YIELD: **4 SERVINGS**

ACTIVE TIME: **20 MINUTES**

TOTAL TIME: **30 MINUTES**

Roman–Style Artichokes

INGREDIENTS

2 LARGE ARTICHOKES

1 LEMON, QUARTERED

VEGETABLE OIL, AS NEEDED

SALT, TO TASTE

LEMON-PEPPER MAYONNAISE
(SEE SIDEBAR), FOR SERVING

DIRECTIONS

1. Prepare the artichokes by using a serrated knife to cut off the top half with the leaves and all but the last inch of the stem; continue whittling away the outer leaves until you see the hairy-looking choke within.

2. Using a paring knife, peel the outer layer of the remaining part of the stem; cut the remaining artichoke into quarters and remove the hairy part in the middle. You should have the heart with a little bit of lower leaves left. Place in a bowl of water, add a squeeze of lemon juice, and set aside.

3. Bring water to a boil in a small saucepan. Add the artichokes and parboil until they begin to feel tender, about 3 to 5 minutes. Remove from the water and drain.

4. Place another small pot on the stove and fill with enough oil that the artichoke hearts will be submerged. Warm the oil over medium heat until it starts to sizzle.

5. Place the artichokes in the oil and fry until they are brown all over, turning occasionally, 8 to 10 minutes. Transfer to a paper towel–lined plate to drain. Season with salt and serve with the Lemon-Pepper Mayonnaise.

YIELD: **1½ CUPS**

ACTIVE TIME: **10 MINUTES**

TOTAL TIME: **10 MINUTES**

Traditional Hummus

INGREDIENTS

1 (14 OZ.) CAN OF CHICKPEAS

3 TABLESPOONS OLIVE OIL

3 TABLESPOONS TAHINI DRESSING
(SEE PAGE 35)

1½ TABLESPOONS FRESH LEMON
JUICE, PLUS MORE TO TASTE

1 GARLIC CLOVE, CHOPPED

1 TEASPOON KOSHER SALT

½ TEASPOON BLACK PEPPER

DIRECTIONS

1. Drain the chickpeas and reserve the liquid. If time allows, remove the skins from each of the chickpeas. This will make your hummus much smoother.

2. Place the chickpeas, olive oil, Tahini Dressing, lemon juice, garlic, salt, and pepper in a food processor and blitz until the mixture is very smooth, scraping down the work bowl as needed.

3. Taste and adjust the seasoning. If your hummus is more stiff than you'd like, add 2 to 3 tablespoons of the reserved chickpea liquid and blitz until it is the desired consistency.

HUMMUS VARIATIONS

For a more authentic hummus, soak dried chickpeas overnight and then cook them for 1 hour. You can also dress it up with any of the following options: add 1 to 3 teaspoons of spices like cumin, sumac, harissa, or smoked paprika; blend in 1 cup of roasted eggplant, zucchini, bell peppers, or garlic; or fold in ¾ cup of chopped green or black olives.

CHAPTER 2

SALADS & SIDES

In order to get your vegetable consumption up to where it needs to be to keep cravings to a minimum when going Mediterranean, and with the limited time modern life leaves for preparation, it's crucial to find a few salads one can comfortably turn to in a pinch. There's no shortage of those here, and there's even a few, like the Couscous & Shrimp Salad on page 70, that can comfortably serve as the evening's entree.

For the nights when you can afford to spend a little more time in the kitchen, we've also included a number of delicious sides that are well worth the extra effort, and a few sauces that can be used to revitalize the other dishes in this book.

Horiatiki Salad

INGREDIENTS

1 CUCUMBER, PEELED, SEEDED,
AND SLICED INTO HALF-MOONS

1 CUP CHERRY TOMATOES, HALVED

1 CUP CRUMBLED FETA CHEESE

1 ONION, CHOPPED

½ CUP KALAMATA OLIVES,
PITTED AND SLICED

1 TEASPOON DRIED OREGANO

½ CUP OLIVE OIL

SALT AND PEPPER, TO TASTE

DIRECTIONS

1. Place the cucumber, cherry tomatoes, feta, onion, olives, and dried oregano in a mixing bowl and stir gently until combined.

2. Drizzle the olive oil over the salad, season with salt and pepper, and gently toss to combine.

YIELD: **4 SERVINGS**

ACTIVE TIME: **5 MINUTES**

TOTAL TIME: **5 MINUTES**

Carrot & Mint Salad

INGREDIENTS

3 CARROTS, PEELED
AND JULIENNED

1 TABLESPOON OLIVE OIL

1 TABLESPOON APPLE
CIDER VINEGAR

¾ TEASPOON CUMIN

2 TABLESPOONS FINELY
CHOPPED FRESH MINT

SALT AND PEPPER, TO TASTE

DIRECTIONS

1. Place all of the ingredients in a mixing bowl and stir gently until combined.

Lentil Salad

INGREDIENTS

4 CUPS WATER

1 CUP LENTILS, PICKED OVER
AND RINSED

2½ TABLESPOONS WHITE
WINE VINEGAR

3 GARLIC CLOVES, MINCED

1 TEASPOON HERBES DE PROVENCE

1 BAY LEAF

SALT AND PEPPER, TO TASTE

1 (14 OZ.) CAN OF CHICKPEAS,
DRAINED AND RINSED

¾ LB. CHERRY TOMATOES, HALVED

1 RED ONION, SLICED

½ CUP FRESH PARSLEY, CHOPPED

¼ CUP OLIVE OIL

2 CUPS BABY SPINACH

½ CUP CRUMBLED FETA CHEESE

DIRECTIONS

1. Place the water, lentils, 1 tablespoon of the vinegar, the garlic, herbes de Provence, and bay leaf in a slow cooker and season with salt. Cover and cook on high until the lentils are tender, about 2 hours.

2. Drain the lentils, discard the bay leaf, transfer to a large salad bowl, and let the lentils cool. Stir in all of the remaining ingredients, except for the feta and pepper, and toss to combine. Season with salt and pepper, sprinkle the feta on top of the salad, and serve.

Charred Brassica Salad with Buttermilk Dressing

YIELD: **4 SERVINGS**

ACTIVE TIME: **20 MINUTES**

TOTAL TIME: **45 MINUTES**

INGREDIENTS

FOR THE SALAD

1 SMALL HEAD OF CAULIFLOWER, TRIMMED AND CHOPPED

1 HEAD OF BROCCOLI, TRIMMED AND CHOPPED

¼ CUP OLIVE OIL

4 OZ. BRUSSELS SPROUTS, TRIMMED AND HALVED

PICKLED RAMPS (SEE SIDEBAR)

RED PEPPER FLAKES, FOR GARNISH

PARMESAN CHEESE, GRATED, FOR GARNISH

Continued...

DIRECTIONS

1. To begin preparations for the salad, bring a large pot of water to a boil. Add the cauliflower, cook for 1 minute, remove with a slotted spoon, and transfer to a paper towel–lined plate. Wait for the water to return to a boil, add the broccoli, and cook for 30 seconds. Use a slotted spoon to remove the broccoli and let the water drip off before transferring it to the paper towel–lined plate.

2. Place the oil and Brussels sprouts, cut side down, in a large cast-iron skillet. Add the broccoli and cauliflower, season with salt and pepper, and cook over high heat without moving the vegetables. Cook until charred, turn over, and cook until charred on that side. Remove and transfer to a salad bowl.

3. To prepare the dressing, place all of the ingredients in a food processor and puree until combined. Taste and adjust the seasoning as needed.

4. Add the Pickled Ramps and dressing to the salad bowl and toss to evenly coat. Garnish with Parmesan cheese and red pepper flakes.

PICKLED RAMPS

Place ½ cup champagne vinegar, ½ cup water, ¼ cup sugar, 1½ teaspoons kosher salt, ¼ teaspoon fennel seeds, ¼ teaspoon coriander seeds, and ⅛ teaspoon red pepper flakes in a small saucepan and bring to a boil. Add 10 small ramp bulbs, reduce heat, and simmer for 1 minute. Transfer the contents of the saucepan to a mason jar, cover, and let cool completely before using or storing in the refrigerator, where they will keep for up to 1 week.

FOR THE DRESSING

2 GARLIC CLOVES, MINCED

1 TEASPOON MISO PASTE

⅔ CUP MAYONNAISE

¼ CUP BUTTERMILK

¼ CUP GRATED PARMESAN CHEESE

ZEST OF 1 LEMON

1 TEASPOON WORCESTERSHIRE SAUCE

1 TEASPOON KOSHER SALT, PLUS MORE TO TASTE

½ TEASPOON BLACK PEPPER, PLUS MORE TO TASTE

YIELD: **4 SERVINGS**

ACTIVE TIME: **20 MINUTES**

TOTAL TIME: **24 HOURS**

Chickpea Salad

INGREDIENTS

2 CUPS DRIED CHICKPEAS,
SOAKED OVERNIGHT

4 CUPS CHICKEN STOCK
(SEE PAGE 108)

1 ONION, CHOPPED

1 CUP FINELY CHOPPED
FRESH CILANTRO

½ CUP SUN-DRIED TOMATOES
IN OLIVE OIL, DRAINED

¼ CUP OLIVE OIL

¼ CUP FRESH LEMON JUICE

¼ TEASPOON SAFFRON

1 TABLESPOON CUMIN

1 TEASPOON CINNAMON

1 TEASPOON RED PEPPER FLAKES

SALT AND PEPPER, TO TASTE

DIRECTIONS

1. Drain the chickpeas, place them in a saucepan, and add the stock. Bring to a boil, reduce the heat, and simmer until the chickpeas are tender, about 40 minutes.

2. Drain the chickpeas and let them cool completely.

3. Place the chickpeas and the remaining ingredients in a small mixing bowl, toss until combined, and serve.

Peppers Stuffed with Feta, Olive & Basil Salad

YIELD: **4 SERVINGS**

ACTIVE TIME: **10 MINUTES**

TOTAL TIME: **25 MINUTES**

INGREDIENTS

4 YELLOW BELL PEPPERS, SEEDED AND HALVED

12 CHERRY TOMATOES, HALVED

2 GARLIC CLOVES, MINCED

2 TABLESPOONS OLIVE OIL

½ CUP CRUMBLED FETA CHEESE

1 CUP BLACK OLIVES, PITTED

SALT AND PEPPER, TO TASTE

LEAVES FROM 1 BUNCH OF FRESH BASIL

DIRECTIONS

1. Preheat the oven to 375°F and place the peppers on a parchment-lined baking sheet.

2. Place the cherry tomatoes, garlic, olive oil, feta, and black olives in a mixing bowl and stir to combine. Divide the mixture between the peppers, place them in the oven, and roast until the peppers start to collapse, 10 to 15 minutes.

3. Remove the peppers from the oven and let cool slightly. Season with salt and pepper and top with the basil leaves before serving.

Three-Bean Salad

INGREDIENTS

FOR THE SALAD

1 (14 OZ.) CAN OF KIDNEY BEANS, DRAINED AND RINSED

1 (14 OZ.) CAN OF CANNELLINI BEANS, DRAINED AND RINSED

1 (14 OZ.) CAN OF CHICKPEAS, DRAINED AND RINSED

1 GREEN BELL PEPPER, STEMMED, SEEDS AND RIBS REMOVED, AND CHOPPED

1 RED BELL PEPPER, STEMMED, SEEDS AND RIBS REMOVED, AND CHOPPED

½ CUCUMBER, CHOPPED

1 RED ONION, CHOPPED

1 CUP FRESH PARSLEY, CHOPPED

10 FRESH MINT LEAVES, TORN

10 FRESH BASIL LEAVES, TORN

FOR THE VINAIGRETTE

2 GARLIC CLOVES, MINCED

1½ TEASPOONS DIJON MUSTARD

2 TABLESPOONS FRESH LEMON JUICE

¼ CUP OLIVE OIL

SALT AND PEPPER, TO TASTE

DIRECTIONS

1. To prepare the salad, place all of the ingredients in a large salad bowl and toss to combine.

2. To prepare the vinaigrette, place all of the ingredients in a small bowl and whisk until combined.

3. Add the vinaigrette to the salad, toss to combine, and serve.

Watermelon & Feta Salad

INGREDIENTS

FOR THE SALAD

FLESH OF ½ WATERMELON, CUBED

1 CUCUMBER, DICED

15 FRESH MINT LEAVES, TORN

15 FRESH BASIL LEAVES, TORN

½ CUP CRUMBLED FETA CHEESE

FOR THE VINAIGRETTE

2 TABLESPOONS HONEY

2 TABLESPOONS FRESH
LEMON JUICE

1 TABLESPOON OLIVE OIL

SALT, TO TASTE

DIRECTIONS

1. To begin preparations for the salad, place all of the ingredients, except for the feta, in a salad bowl and toss to combine.

2. To prepare the vinaigrette, place all of the ingredients in a mixing bowl and whisk vigorously until combined.

3. Add the vinaigrette to the salad, gently toss to combine, and top with the feta.

Mediterranean Tuna Salad

YIELD: **4 SERVINGS**

ACTIVE TIME: **25 MINUTES**

TOTAL TIME: **25 MINUTES**

INGREDIENTS

3 (5 OZ.) CANS OF TUNA IN OLIVE OIL, DRAINED

3 CELERY STALKS, DICED

½ CUCUMBER, DICED

1 RED BELL PEPPER, STEMMED, SEEDS AND RIBS REMOVED, AND DICED

3 SCALLIONS, TRIMMED AND DICED

½ RED ONION, DICED

1 CUP FRESH PARSLEY, CHOPPED

10 FRESH MINT LEAVES, FINELY CHOPPED

SALT AND PEPPER, TO TASTE

1 TEASPOON DIJON MUSTARD

½ TABLESPOON MINCED SHALLOT

2 TABLESPOONS WHITE WINE VINEGAR

⅓ CUP OLIVE OIL

½ TEASPOON SUMAC POWDER

½ TEASPOON RED PEPPER FLAKES

PITA BREAD (SEE PAGE 31), FOR SERVING (OPTIONAL)

5 OZ. MESCLUN GREENS, FOR SERVING (OPTIONAL)

DIRECTIONS

1. Place the tuna in a mixing bowl and incorporate the celery, cucumber, bell pepper, scallions, onion, parsley, and mint leaves one at a time. Season the mixture with salt and pepper and set it aside.

2. Place the remaining ingredients in a separate bowl and stir to combine. Add the dressing to the tuna salad, stir to combine, and serve with Pita Bread or over mesclun greens.

Couscous & Shrimp Salad

YIELD: **6 SERVINGS**

ACTIVE TIME: **40 MINUTES**

TOTAL TIME: **50 MINUTES**

INGREDIENTS

¾ LB. SHRIMP, SHELLED AND DEVEINED

6 BUNCHES OF FRESH MINT

10 GARLIC CLOVES, PEELED

3½ CUPS CHICKEN STOCK (SEE PAGE 108)

3 CUPS ISRAELI COUSCOUS

1 BUNCH OF ASPARAGUS, TRIMMED

3 PLUM TOMATOES, DICED

1 TABLESPOON FINELY CHOPPED FRESH OREGANO

½ ENGLISH CUCUMBER, DICED

ZEST AND JUICE OF 1 LEMON

½ CUP DICED RED ONION

½ CUP SUN-DRIED TOMATOES IN OLIVE OIL, DRAINED AND SLICED THIN

¼ CUP PITTED AND CHOPPED KALAMATA OLIVES

⅓ CUP OLIVE OIL

SALT AND PEPPER, TO TASTE

½ CUP CRUMBLED FETA CHEESE

DIRECTIONS

1. Place the shrimp, mint, and garlic in a Dutch oven and cover with water. Bring to a simmer over medium heat and cook until the shrimp are pink and cooked through, about 4 minutes after the water comes to a simmer. Drain, cut the shrimp in half lengthwise, and them set aside. Discard the mint and garlic cloves.

2. Place the stock in the Dutch oven and bring to a boil. Add the couscous, reduce the heat so that the stock simmers, cover, and cook until the couscous is tender and has absorbed the stock, 7 to 10 minutes. Transfer the couscous to a salad bowl.

3. Fill the pot with water and bring it to a boil. Add the asparagus and cook until it has softened, 1 to 1½ minutes. Drain, rinse under cold water, and chop into bite-sized pieces. Pat the asparagus dry.

4. Add all of the remaining ingredients, except for the feta, to the salad bowl containing the couscous. Add the asparagus and stir to incorporate. Top with the shrimp and the feta and serve.

Panzanella with White Balsamic Vinaigrette

YIELD: **6 SERVINGS**

ACTIVE TIME: **25 MINUTES**

TOTAL TIME: **45 MINUTES**

INGREDIENTS

FOR THE SALAD

1 TABLESPOON KOSHER SALT, PLUS 2 TEASPOONS

6 PEARL ONIONS, TRIMMED

1 CUP CORN KERNELS

1 CUP CHOPPED GREEN BEANS

4 CUPS CHOPPED DAY-OLD BREAD

2 CUPS CHOPPED OVERRIPE TOMATOES

10 LARGE FRESH BASIL LEAVES, TORN

BLACK PEPPER, TO TASTE

FOR THE VINAIGRETTE

½ CUP WHITE BALSAMIC VINEGAR

¼ CUP OLIVE OIL

2 TABLESPOONS MINCED SHALLOT

¼ CUP SLICED SCALLIONS

2 TABLESPOONS FINELY CHOPPED FRESH PARSLEY

2 TEASPOONS KOSHER SALT

1 TEASPOON BLACK PEPPER

DIRECTIONS

1. To begin preparations for the salad, bring water to a boil in a small saucepan and prepare an ice water bath. When the water is boiling, add the 1 tablespoon of salt and the pearl onions and cook for 5 minutes. When the onions have 1 minute left to cook, add the corn and green beans to the saucepan. Transfer the vegetables to the ice water bath and let them cool completely.

2. Remove the pearl onions from the water and squeeze to remove the bulbs from their skins. Cut the bulbs in half and break them down into individual petals. Drain the corn and green beans and pat the vegetables dry.

3. To prepare the vinaigrette, place all of the ingredients in a mixing bowl and whisk until combined.

4. Place the cooked vegetables, bread, tomatoes, and basil in a salad bowl and toss to combine. Add the remaining salt, season with pepper, and add half of the vinaigrette. Toss to coat, taste, and add more of the vinaigrette if desired.

YIELD: **1½ CUPS**

ACTIVE TIME: **25 MINUTES**

TOTAL TIME: **35 MINUTES**

Harissa Sauce

INGREDIENTS

1 HABANERO PEPPER

¾ TEASPOON CARAWAY SEEDS

¾ TEASPOON CORIANDER SEEDS

1½ TEASPOONS CUMIN SEEDS

1½ TEASPOONS DRIED MINT

1 TABLESPOON KOSHER SALT, PLUS MORE TO TASTE

12 GARLIC CLOVES

JUICE OF 3 LEMONS

3 TABLESPOONS OLIVE OIL

1 CUP GREEK YOGURT

1 TEASPOON FINELY CHOPPED FRESH CILANTRO

1 TEASPOON FINELY CHOPPED FRESH MINT

1 TEASPOON FINELY CHOPPED FRESH PARSLEY

1 TEASPOON FINELY CHOPPED FRESH CHIVES

BLACK PEPPER, TO TASTE

DIRECTIONS

1. Hold the habanero over an open flame on your stove or under the broiler. Roast, while turning, until all sides of the pepper are charred. Place the pepper in a bowl, cover the bowl with plastic wrap, and let it cool for 10 minutes. Remove the stem, skin, and seeds from the pepper (gloves are recommended while handling the habanero) and discard them. Mince the habanero's flesh and set it aside.

2. Place the seeds in a dry skillet and toast them over medium heat, shaking the pan frequently, until the seeds begin to release their aroma. Remove the seeds from the pan and let them cool. When cool, grind the seeds into a fine powder, using either a spice grinder or a mortar and pestle.

3. Place the remaining ingredients, the roasted habanero, and the toasted seed powder in a food processor, blitz until smooth, and use as desired.

YIELD: **6 SERVINGS**

ACTIVE TIME: **10 MINUTES**

TOTAL TIME: **35 MINUTES**

Honey-Glazed Carrots

INGREDIENTS

1 TABLESPOON OLIVE OIL

2 TABLESPOONS HONEY

1 TEASPOON CUMIN

¼ TEASPOON GROUND GINGER

½ TEASPOON CINNAMON

4 CARROTS, PEELED AND CHOPPED

SALT AND PEPPER, TO TASTE

DIRECTIONS

1. Preheat the oven to 400°F. Place the olive oil, honey, cumin, ginger, and cinnamon in a bowl and stir to combine. Add the carrots and toss to coat.

2. Place the carrots on a parchment-lined baking sheet and season with salt and pepper. Place the carrots in the oven and roast for about 20 minutes, or until tender and lightly browned. Remove from the oven and let cool briefly before serving.

Brussels Sprouts with Lemon, Olive Oil & Hazelnuts

YIELD: **4 SERVINGS**

ACTIVE TIME: **15 MINUTES**

TOTAL TIME: **20 MINUTES**

INGREDIENTS

¼ CUP HAZELNUTS

½ LB. BRUSSELS SPROUTS, TRIMMED AND SLICED VERY THIN

⅓ CUP OLIVE OIL

1 TABLESPOON FRESH LEMON JUICE

1 TEASPOON REAL MAPLE SYRUP

SALT, TO TASTE

DIRECTIONS

1. Place the hazelnuts in a large, dry skillet and toast over medium heat until they just start to brown, about 5 minutes. Transfer the nuts to a clean, dry kitchen towel, fold the towel over the nuts, and rub them together until the skins have loosened. Remove the cleaned nuts and discard the skins. Roughly chop the toasted hazelnuts.

2. Place the Brussels sprouts in a salad bowl and drizzle the olive oil, lemon juice, maple syrup over the top. Season with salt, add the hazelnuts, toss to combine, and serve.

NOTE: For best results, use a mandoline to slice the Brussels sprouts.

Charred Eggplant with Feta

YIELD: **4 SERVINGS**

ACTIVE TIME: **5 MINUTES**

TOTAL TIME: **30 MINUTES**

INGREDIENTS

2 LARGE EGGPLANTS

SALT AND PEPPER, TO TASTE

2 TABLESPOONS OLIVE OIL

1 TABLESPOON BALSAMIC GLAZE

¼ CUP CRUMBLED FETA CHEESE

RED PEPPER FLAKES, TO TASTE

1 TABLESPOON FINELY CHOPPED
FRESH OREGANO

DIRECTIONS

1. Set the oven's broiler to high. Place the eggplants in a 12-inch cast-iron skillet and place the pan under the broiler. Broil, while turning occasionally, until the eggplants have collapsed and are charred all over, about 10 minutes. Remove from the oven, transfer the eggplants to a large bowl, and cover the bowl with plastic wrap. Let the eggplants steam for 10 minutes.

2. When the eggplants are cool enough to handle, peel off the skin, cut off the ends, and discard. Roughly chop the remaining flesh and return it to the large bowl. Add the remaining ingredients, stir to combine, and serve immediately.

Lemon Cauliflower Rice

INGREDIENTS

1 HEAD OF CAULIFLOWER, CHOPPED

2 TABLESPOONS OLIVE OIL

SALT, TO TASTE

3 TABLESPOONS FRESH LEMON JUICE

2 TEASPOONS LEMON ZEST

DIRECTIONS

1. Place the pieces of cauliflower in a food processor and blitz until granular.

2. Place the olive oil in a skillet and warm it over medium-high heat. When the oil starts to shimmer, add the cauliflower and cook, stirring occasionally, until it starts to brown, about 8 minutes.

3. Season with salt, stir in the lemon juice and lemon zest and cook, stirring occasionally, until the "rice" is fragrant and warmed through, about 4 minutes.

Roasted Roots with Ras el Hanout & Honey

YIELD: **4 SERVINGS**

ACTIVE TIME: **10 MINUTES**

TOTAL TIME: **45 MINUTES**

INGREDIENTS

4 LARGE PARSNIPS, PEELED, TRIMMED, CORED, AND CHOPPED

4 LARGE CARROTS, PEELED AND SLICED LENGTHWISE

2 TABLESPOONS OLIVE OIL

SALT AND PEPPER, TO TASTE

2 TABLESPOONS HONEY

1 TABLESPOON RAS EL HANOUT

DIRECTIONS

1. Preheat the oven to 400°F. Place the parsnips and carrots in a roasting pan in one layer, drizzle the olive oil over the top, and season with salt and pepper. Stir to combine, place the pan in the oven, and roast for about 25 minutes, or until the vegetables are starting to brown.

2. Remove the pan from the oven and move the vegetables into a pile in the center of the tray. Drizzle the honey over the pile and stir until the vegetables are evenly coated. Sprinkle the Ras el Hanout over the vegetables and stir until evenly distributed.

3. Return the pan to the oven and roast the vegetables for another 5 to 10 minutes, until the vegetables are well browned and cooked through. Remove from the oven and let the vegetables cool briefly before serving.

YIELD: **4 SERVINGS**

ACTIVE TIME: **25 MINUTES**

TOTAL TIME: **40 MINUTES**

Taro Ulass

INGREDIENTS

½ CUP VEGETABLE STOCK
(SEE PAGE 103)

JUICE FROM ½ LEMON

1 LB. TARO ROOT, PEELED
AND CUBED

1 LARGE BUNCH OF RED CHARD,
STEMS AND LEAVES SEPARATED
AND CHOPPED

½ BUNCH OF FRESH CILANTRO,
CHOPPED

1 TABLESPOON OLIVE OIL

2 GARLIC CLOVES, CHOPPED

DIRECTIONS

1. Place the stock, lemon juice, and taro in a saucepan, bring to a simmer over medium heat, and cook until the taro is tender, about 8 minutes. Remove the pan from heat and set it aside.

2. Place the chard leaves and the cilantro in a pan containing approximately ¼ cup water. Cook over medium heat until the chard is wilted and most of the liquid has evaporated. Transfer the mixture to a food processor and blitz until pureed.

3. Place the olive oil in a large skillet and warm over medium heat. When the oil starts to shimmer, add the garlic and the chard stems and sauté until the garlic starts to brown slightly, about 1 minute. Stir in the taro mixture and the chard puree, cook until heated through, and serve.

YIELD: **4 CUPS**

ACTIVE TIME: **15 MINUTES**

TOTAL TIME: **30 MINUTES**

Tabbouleh

INGREDIENTS

½ CUP BULGUR WHEAT

1½ CUPS BOILING WATER

½ TEASPOON KOSHER SALT,
PLUS MORE TO TASTE

½ CUP FRESH LEMON JUICE

2 CUPS FRESH PARSLEY, CHOPPED

1 CUP PEELED, SEEDED, AND
DICED CUCUMBER

2 TOMATOES, DICED

6 SCALLIONS, TRIMMED

1 CUP FRESH MINT LEAVES,
CHOPPED

2 TABLESPOONS OLIVE OIL

BLACK PEPPER, TO TASTE

½ CUP CRUMBLED FETA CHEESE

DIRECTIONS

1. Place the bulgur in a heatproof bowl and add the boiling water, salt, and half of the lemon juice. Cover and let sit for about 20 minutes, until the bulgur has absorbed all of the liquid and is tender. Drain any excess liquid if necessary. Let the bulgur cool completely.

2. When the bulgur has completely cooled, add the parsley, cucumber, tomatoes, scallions, mint, olive oil, black pepper, and remaining lemon juice. Top with the feta and serve.

Roasted Beans with Mint & Feta

YIELD: **4 SERVINGS**

ACTIVE TIME: **15 MINUTES**

TOTAL TIME: **45 MINUTES**

INGREDIENTS

¾ LB. FRESH GREEN BEANS, TRIMMED

¾ LB. FRESH WAX BEANS, TRIMMED

3 TABLESPOONS OLIVE OIL

¾ TEASPOON ALLSPICE

PINCH OF CAYENNE PEPPER

1 TEASPOON KOSHER SALT

¼ TEASPOON BLACK PEPPER

1 CUP CHERRY TOMATOES, HALVED

2 TABLESPOONS FINELY CHOPPED FRESH MINT

1 TABLESPOON RED WINE VINEGAR

½ CUP CRUMBLED FETA CHEESE

DIRECTIONS

1. Preheat the oven to 400°F. Place the beans in a large mixing bowl, add the olive oil, allspice, cayenne, salt, and pepper, and stir until the beans are evenly coated.

2. Place the beans in a baking dish, place it in the oven, and roast until the beans are al dente, 20 to 25 minutes. Remove from the oven and return them to the large mixing bowl.

3. Add the tomatoes, mint, vinegar, and feta, stir to combine, and serve.

Asparagus with Tahini Dressing, Three Ways

YIELD: **4 SERVINGS**

ACTIVE TIME: **10 MINUTES**

TOTAL TIME: **10 MINUTES**

INGREDIENTS

1½ LBS. ASPARAGUS

OLIVE OIL, TO TASTE

SALT, TO TASTE

TAHINI DRESSING (SEE PAGE 35), FOR SERVING

DIRECTIONS

1. Begin every preparation for asparagus by rinsing the spears well under cold water. Take a spear and bend it close to the end that is opposite the pointy tip; it will snap off at the point where it starts to be too fibrous and tough to eat. Discard the fibrous ends.

2. To blanch asparagus, place the spears in salted, boiling water for about 3 minutes, or just tender. Transfer immediately to an ice water bath to retain the bright green color.

3. To steam asparagus, arrange the spears in a steaming tray, place the tray above 1 inch of boiling water, and steam for roughly 5 minutes. Transfer immediately to an ice water bath to retain the bright green color.

4. To grill asparagus, preheat your grill to medium-high heat (450°F). Place the asparagus in a bowl, drizzle some olive oil over it, and season with salt. Toss to coat, place the asparagus on the grill, and cook until it just starts to char, about 4 minutes. Turn over, cook for another 4 minutes, then transfer to a plate.

5. Serve any of these preparations with the Tahini Dressing and season to taste.

YIELD: **4 SERVINGS**

ACTIVE TIME: **15 MINUTES**

TOTAL TIME: **40 MINUTES**

Bamies

INGREDIENTS

OLIVE OIL, AS NEEDED

1 ONION, CHOPPED

1 LB. OKRA, RINSED WELL
AND CHOPPED

1 POTATO, MINCED

1 GARLIC CLOVE, MINCED

2 TOMATOES, CHOPPED

3 TABLESPOONS WHITE WINE

½ CUP VEGETABLE STOCK
(SEE PAGE 103)

2 TABLESPOONS FINELY CHOPPED
FRESH PARSLEY

2 TEASPOONS SUGAR

SALT, TO TASTE

FETA CHEESE, CRUMBLED,
FOR GARNISH

DIRECTIONS

1. Place the oil in a 10-inch skillet and warm over medium heat. When the oil starts to shimmer, add the onion and sauté until it starts to brown, about 8 minutes. Add the okra and potato and cook, stirring continuously, until they start to brown, about 5 minutes.

2. Add the garlic and cook for 1 minute. Add the tomatoes, wine, stock, parsley, and sugar and stir to incorporate. Cook until the tomatoes have completely collapsed and the okra and potato are tender, about 8 minutes. Season with salt, garnish with feta, and serve immediately.

YIELD: **1½ CUPS**

ACTIVE TIME: **5 MINUTES**

TOTAL TIME: **5 MINUTES**

Romesco Sauce

INGREDIENTS

2 LARGE ROASTED RED
BELL PEPPERS

1 GARLIC CLOVE, SMASHED

½ CUP SLIVERED ALMONDS OR
CHOPPED HAZELNUTS, TOASTED

¼ CUP PUREED TOMATOES

2 TABLESPOONS FINELY CHOPPED
FRESH PARSLEY

2 TABLESPOONS SHERRY VINEGAR

1 TEASPOON SMOKED PAPRIKA

SALT AND PEPPER, TO TASTE

½ CUP OLIVE OIL

DIRECTIONS

1. Place all of the ingredients, except for the olive oil, in
    a blender or food processor and pulse until the mixture
    is smooth.

2. Add the olive oil in a steady stream and blitz until emulsified.
    Taste, adjust the seasoning as necessary, and use as desired.

CHAPTER 3

SOUPS &
STEWS

---

*Able to provide comfort when the world turns chilly.
Freighted with enough flavor and intrigue to be proudly presented
to company. Either ready in no time at all or requiring little
hands-on engagement, effortlessly developing flavor
as you proceed with the demands of the day.*

*When you take all of this into account, the recipes that
make up this chapter may very well be the best in the book—
both bursting with the unique tastes that exist throughout the
Mediterranean region, and allowing you to easily remain
on track in your move toward a healthier lifestyle.*

YIELD: **4 SERVINGS**

ACTIVE TIME: **30 MINUTES**

TOTAL TIME: **1 HOUR AND 15 MINUTES**

Minestrone

INGREDIENTS

2 TABLESPOONS OLIVE OIL

1 GARLIC CLOVE, MINCED

2 ONIONS, MINCED

2 CARROTS, PEELED AND MINCED

1 LEEK, WHITE PART ONLY, MINCED

2 YELLOW BELL PEPPERS, STEMMED, SEEDS AND RIBS REMOVED, AND MINCED

2 RED BELL PEPPERS, STEMMED, SEEDS AND RIBS REMOVED, AND MINCED

2 ZUCCHINI, MINCED

8 CHERRY TOMATOES, CHOPPED

6 CUPS TOMATO JUICE

½ TEASPOON FINELY CHOPPED FRESH THYME

½ TEASPOON FINELY CHOPPED FRESH ROSEMARY

SALT AND PEPPER, TO TASTE

PARMESAN CHEESE, SHAVED, FOR GARNISH

DIRECTIONS

1. Place the oil in a large saucepan and warm over medium heat. When the oil starts to shimmer, add the garlic, onions, carrots, and leek and sauté until the vegetables start to soften, about 5 minutes.

2. Add the peppers, cook for 5 minutes, and then stir in the zucchini and cherry tomatoes. Cook for 3 minutes, add the tomato juice, thyme, and rosemary, and bring to a boil.

3. Reduce the heat so that the soup simmers and cook until the vegetables are tender, about 20 minutes. Season with salt and pepper, ladle into warmed bowls, and garnish with the Parmesan.

Go for the Green Stew

INGREDIENTS

1 TABLESPOON OLIVE OIL

1 ONION, CHOPPED

2 GARLIC CLOVES, MINCED

1 CELERY STALK, MINCED

1 GREEN BELL PEPPER,
STEMMED, SEEDS AND RIBS
REMOVED, AND CHOPPED

¼ HEAD OF GREEN CABBAGE,
CORED AND SLICED THIN

½ TEASPOON FINELY CHOPPED
FRESH OREGANO

½ TEASPOON FINELY CHOPPED
FRESH THYME

1 BAY LEAF

6 CUPS VEGETABLE STOCK
(SEE SIDEBAR)

2 CUPS SHREDDED
COLLARD GREENS

2 CUPS SHREDDED BABY SPINACH

1 BUNCH OF WATERCRESS

12 OZ. TOFU, DRAINED AND
CHOPPED INTO ¼-INCH PIECES

¼ CUP FINELY CHOPPED
FRESH PARSLEY

½ TEASPOON ALLSPICE

PINCH OF CAYENNE PEPPER

SALT AND PEPPER, TO TASTE

DIRECTIONS

1. Place the olive oil in a large saucepan and warm over medium heat. When the oil starts to shimmer, add the onion, garlic, celery, and bell pepper and sauté until the onion and celery start to soften, about 5 minutes.

2. Stir in the cabbage, oregano, thyme, and bay leaf, cook for 5 minutes, and then add the stock. Bring the stew to a boil, reduce heat so that it simmers, and cook for 5 minutes.

3. Stir in the collard greens and cook for 5 minutes. Add the spinach, watercress, and tofu and cook for 2 minutes before adding the parsley, allspice, and cayenne. Season with salt and pepper, simmer for 2 more minutes, and ladle into warmed bowls.

VEGETABLE STOCK

Place 2 tablespoons olive oil, 2 trimmed and well rinsed leeks, 2 peeled and sliced carrots, 2 celery stalks, 2 sliced onions, and 3 unpeeled, smashed garlic cloves in a large stockpot and cook over low heat until the liquid the vegetables release has evaporated. Add 2 sprigs of fresh parsley and thyme, 1 bay leaf, 8 cups water, ½ teaspoon black peppercorns, and salt to taste. Raise the heat to high and bring the stock to a boil. Reduce heat so that the stock simmers and cook for 2 hours, skimming to remove any impurities that float to the surface. Strain the stock through a fine sieve, let the stock cool slightly, and place it in the refrigerator, uncovered, to chill. Remove the fat layer and cover. The stock will keep in the refrigerator for 3 to 5 days, and in the freezer for up to 3 months.

Dried Fava Bean Soup with Grilled Halloumi Cheese

YIELD: **4 SERVINGS**

ACTIVE TIME: **30 MINUTES**

TOTAL TIME: **24 HOURS**

INGREDIENTS

1½ CUPS DRIED FAVA BEANS, SOAKED OVERNIGHT

6 CUPS VEGETABLE STOCK (SEE PAGE 103)

4 GARLIC CLOVES, MINCED

5 TABLESPOONS OLIVE OIL

1 SHALLOT, MINCED

ZEST AND JUICE OF 1 LEMON

SALT AND PEPPER, TO TASTE

2 TABLESPOONS FINELY CHOPPED FRESH PARSLEY

½ LB. HALLOUMI CHEESE, CUT INTO 4 PIECES

LEMON WEDGES, FOR SERVING

DIRECTIONS

1. Drain the fava beans and place them in a large saucepan with the stock and garlic. Bring to a boil, reduce the heat so that the soup simmers, cover, and cook until the beans are so tender that they are falling apart, about 1 hour.

2. While the soup is simmering, place ¼ cup of the olive oil in a skillet and warm over medium heat. When the oil starts to shimmer, add the shallot and sauté until it starts to soften, about 5 minutes. Remove the pan from heat, stir in the lemon zest, and let the mixture sit for 1 hour.

3. Transfer the soup to a food processor and puree until smooth. Return the soup to a clean saucepan, season with salt and pepper, and bring it to a gentle simmer. Stir in the mixture in the skillet, the lemon juice, and the parsley, cook until heated through, and remove the soup from heat.

4. Warm a skillet over medium heat. Place the remaining olive oil in a small bowl, add the cheese, and toss to coat. Place the cheese in the pan and cook until browned on both sides, about 2 minutes per side. Serve alongside the soup.

Lamb & Lentil Soup

INGREDIENTS

4 CUPS VEGETABLE STOCK
(SEE PAGE 103)

1 LB. LEG OF LAMB, CUT INTO
1-INCH PIECES

1 ONION, MINCED

2 GARLIC CLOVES, MINCED

2 BAY LEAVES

4 WHOLE CLOVES

4 SPRIGS OF FRESH THYME

1 POTATO, PEELED AND CHOPPED

½ CUP RED LENTILS

SALT AND PEPPER, TO TASTE

2 TABLESPOONS FINELY CHOPPED
FRESH PARSLEY

DIRECTIONS

1. Place the stock, lamb, onion, garlic, bay leaves, cloves, and thyme in a large saucepan and bring to a boil over medium-high heat. Reduce the heat to medium-low and simmer the soup until the lamb is tender, about 45 minutes.

2. Remove the sprigs of thyme and the cloves, add the potato and lentils, cover the pan, and cook until the lentils and potato are tender, about 10 minutes.

3. Season with salt and pepper, stir in the parsley, and ladle into warmed bowls.

CHICKEN STOCK

Place 3 lbs. rinsed chicken bones in a large stockpot, cover them with water, and bring to a boil. Add 1 chopped onion, 2 chopped carrots, 3 chopped celery stalks, 3 unpeeled, smashed garlic cloves, 3 sprigs of fresh thyme, 1 teaspoon black peppercorns, 1 bay leaf, season the stock with salt, and reduce the heat so that the stock simmers. Cook for 2 hours, skimming to remove any impurities that float to the surface. Strain the stock through a fine sieve, let the stock cool slightly, and place it in the refrigerator, uncovered, to chill. Remove the fat layer and cover. The stock will keep in the refrigerator for 3 to 5 days, and in the freezer for up to 3 months.

Split Pea Soup with Smoked Ham

YIELD: **4 SERVINGS**

ACTIVE TIME: **30 MINUTES**

TOTAL TIME: **2 HOURS**

INGREDIENTS

2 TABLESPOONS UNSALTED BUTTER

1 ONION, MINCED

1 CARROT, PEELED AND MINCED

1 CELERY STALK, MINCED

5 CUPS CHICKEN STOCK
(SEE SIDEBAR)

1 CUP SPLIT PEAS

½ LB. SMOKED HAM, CHOPPED

2 TABLESPOONS FINELY
CHOPPED FRESH PARSLEY,
PLUS MORE FOR GARNISH

1 BAY LEAF

1 TEASPOON FINELY CHOPPED
FRESH THYME

SALT AND PEPPER, TO TASTE

LEMON WEDGES, FOR SERVING

DIRECTIONS

1. Place the butter in a large saucepan and melt over medium heat. Add the onion, carrot, and celery and sauté until they have softened, about 5 minutes.

2. Add the stock, split peas, ham, parsley, bay leaf, and thyme. Bring the soup to a boil, reduce the heat to medium-low, and simmer, stirring occasionally, until the peas are al dente, about 1 hour.

3. Remove the bay leaf and discard it. Season the soup with salt and pepper and ladle it into warmed bowls. Garnish with additional parsley and serve with lemon wedges.

Chamin

INGREDIENTS

1½ TABLESPOONS OLIVE OIL

1 SMALL ONION, CHOPPED

5 GARLIC CLOVES, MINCED

¾ CUP CHOPPED PARSNIP

2 CARROTS, PEELED AND SLICED

1 TEASPOON CUMIN

¼ TEASPOON TURMERIC

1½-INCH PIECE OF FRESH GINGER, PEELED AND MINCED

½ LB. BEEF BRISKET, TRIMMED AND CHOPPED

4 OZ. LAMB SHOULDER, TRIMMED AND CHOPPED

4 CUPS BEEF STOCK (SEE SIDEBAR)

½ CUP CHICKPEAS, SOAKED OVERNIGHT AND DRAINED

1 SMALL POTATO, PEELED AND CHOPPED

Continued...

DIRECTIONS

1. Preheat the oven to 250°F. Place the olive oil in a Dutch oven and warm over medium heat. Add the onion, garlic, parsnip, carrots, cumin, turmeric, and ginger and sauté for 2 minutes. Add the brisket and lamb and cook, stirring occasionally, until both are browned all over, about 8 minutes.

2. Add the stock and bring the soup to a simmer. Stir in the chickpeas, potato, zucchini, tomatoes, lentils, bay leaf, and cilantro. Cover the pot, place it in the oven, and cook until the meat is tender, about 1 hour.

3. Remove the stew from the oven and skim the fat from the top. Season with salt and pepper and ladle into warmed bowls. Garnish with the chilies and serve with the lemon wedges and rice.

1 SMALL ZUCCHINI, SLICED

½ LB. TOMATOES, CHOPPED

2 TABLESPOONS BROWN LENTILS

1 BAY LEAF

½ BUNCH OF FRESH CILANTRO, CHOPPED

SALT AND PEPPER, TO TASTE

RED CHILI PEPPERS, STEMMED, SEEDS AND RIBS REMOVED, AND CHOPPED, FOR GARNISH

LEMON WEDGES, FOR SERVING

LONG-GRAIN RICE, COOKED, FOR SERVING

YIELD: **4 SERVINGS**

ACTIVE TIME: **20 MINUTES**

TOTAL TIME: **24 HOURS**

Lamb & Cannellini Soup

INGREDIENTS

2 TABLESPOONS OLIVE OIL

1 ONION, CHOPPED

2 GARLIC CLOVES, MINCED

1½ LBS. GROUND LAMB

3 CARROTS, PEELED AND CHOPPED

3 CELERY STALKS, CHOPPED

1 (14 OZ.) CAN OF STEWED
TOMATOES, DRAINED

¼ CUP FINELY CHOPPED FRESH
PARSLEY

2 TABLESPOONS FINELY CHOPPED
FRESH THYME

½ LB. DRIED CANNELLINI
BEANS, SOAKED OVERNIGHT
AND DRAINED

6 CUPS CHICKEN STOCK
(SEE PAGE 108)

½ LB. BABY SPINACH

¼ CUP SLICED KALAMATA OLIVES

SALT AND PEPPER, TO TASTE

FETA CHEESE, CRUMBLED,
FOR GARNISH

DIRECTIONS

1. Place the olive oil in a large saucepan and warm over medium heat. When the oil starts to shimmer, add the onion and sauté until it starts to soften, about 5 minutes. Stir in the garlic, cook for 2 minutes, and then add the lamb. Cook until it starts to brown, about 5 minutes, and add the carrots and celery.

2. Cook for 5 minutes, stir in the tomatoes, herbs, cannellini beans, and stock, and bring the soup to a boil. Reduce the heat to medium-low, cover the pan, and simmer for 1 hour, until the beans are tender.

3. Add the spinach and olives and cook until the spinach wilts, about 2 minutes. Season with salt and pepper, ladle into warmed bowls, and garnish with the feta cheese.

YIELD: **4 SERVINGS**

ACTIVE TIME: **30 MINUTES**

TOTAL TIME: **1 HOUR AND 30 MINUTES**

Mansaf

INGREDIENTS

2 TABLESPOONS OLIVE OIL

1 ONION, CHOPPED

2 LBS. LAMB SHOULDER, CUBED

6 CUPS BEEF STOCK (SEE PAGE 111)

SEEDS FROM 2 CARDAMOM PODS

1 CUP PLAIN GREEK YOGURT

SALT AND PEPPER, TO TASTE

2 CUPS COOKED LONG-GRAIN RICE

¼ CUP PINE NUTS, TOASTED,
FOR GARNISH

FRESH PARSLEY, FINELY CHOPPED,
FOR GARNISH

DIRECTIONS

1. Place the olive oil in a saucepan and warm over medium-high heat. When it starts to shimmer, add the onion and sauté until it starts to soften, about 5 minutes. Add the lamb and cook until it is browned all over, about 8 minutes.

2. Add the stock and cardamom and bring the soup to a boil. Reduce the heat to medium-low, cover the pan, and simmer until the lamb is very tender, about 1 hour.

3. Stir in the yogurt, season with salt and pepper, and remove the soup from heat. Divide the rice between the serving bowls, ladle the soup over the rice, and garnish with the pine nuts and parsley.

Mediterranean Chicken Stew

INGREDIENTS

3 TABLESPOONS UNSALTED BUTTER

2 BONELESS, SKINLESS CHICKEN BREASTS, CHOPPED

1 LARGE ONION, CHOPPED

1 GARLIC CLOVE, MINCED

2 GREEN BELL PEPPERS, STEMMED, SEEDS AND RIBS REMOVED, AND CHOPPED

¼ TEASPOON ALLSPICE

½ TEASPOON GROUND CLOVES

½ TEASPOON CINNAMON

¼ TEASPOON FINELY CHOPPED FRESH THYME, PLUS MORE FOR GARNISH

½ BIRD'S EYE CHILI PEPPER, STEMMED, SEEDS AND RIBS REMOVED, AND MINCED

¼ CUP SLICED KALAMATA OLIVES

Continued...

DIRECTIONS

1. Place 1 tablespoon of the butter in a large saucepan and melt over medium heat. Add the chicken and cook, stirring occasionally, until browned all over, about 8 minutes. Remove from the pan and set the chicken aside.

2. Melt another tablespoon of the butter in the pan, add the onion, garlic, and bell peppers and sauté until they are soft, about 10 minutes. Return the chicken to the pan and add the allspice, cloves, cinnamon, thyme, and chili. Cook, stirring constantly, for 2 minutes.

3. Add the olives and Chicken Stock, reduce the heat to low, and simmer until the chicken is very tender, about 45 minutes.

4. Add the tomatoes, season with salt and pepper, and stir in the remaining butter. Remove the soup from heat.

5. Place the Vegetable Stock in a saucepan and bring to a boil over medium-high heat. Reduce the heat to low and gradually stir in the cornmeal. Cook until tender, about 5 minutes.

6. Stir the kefalotyri into the cornmeal, season with salt and pepper, and divide the mixture between the serving bowls. Ladle the soup over the cornmeal mixture and garnish with the feta and additional thyme.

4 CUPS CHICKEN STOCK
(SEE PAGE 108)

1½ CUPS CHOPPED TOMATOES

SALT AND PEPPER, TO TASTE

1¼ CUPS VEGETABLE STOCK
(SEE PAGE 103)

½ CUP CORNMEAL

1 CUP GRATED KEFALOTYRI CHEESE

FETA CHEESE, CRUMBLED,
FOR GARNISH

SEAFOOD STOCK

Break 2 lobster carcasses into small pieces and place them in a large stockpot. Add the shells from 2 lbs. raw shrimp, 8 cups water, 1 cup dry white wine, 1 peeled and chopped carrot, 1 sliced onion, 1 sliced celery stalk, 1 tablespoon black peppercorns, 3 sprigs of fresh parsley and thyme, 2 unpeeled, smashed garlic cloves, and 1 bay leaf and bring to a boil over high heat. Reduce the heat to low and simmer the stock for 1½ hours, skimming to remove any impurities that rise to the surface. Strain the stock through a fine sieve, let it cool slightly, and place it in the refrigerator, uncovered, to chill. Remove the fat layer and cover. The stock will keep in the refrigerator for up to 5 days, and in the freezer for up to 3 months.

YIELD: **6 SERVINGS**

ACTIVE TIME: **25 MINUTES**

TOTAL TIME: **1 HOUR**

Bouillabaisse

INGREDIENTS

6 TABLESPOONS OLIVE OIL

1 ONION, CHOPPED

½ LEEK, WHITE PART ONLY, SLICED

1 CELERY STALK, CHOPPED

1 CUP CHOPPED FENNEL

2 GARLIC CLOVES, MINCED

1 SPRIG OF FRESH THYME

1 BAY LEAF

ZEST OF 1 ORANGE

1 TOMATO, CHOPPED

PINCH OF SAFFRON

3 CUPS FISH STOCK (SEE PAGE 141)

3 CUPS SEAFOOD STOCK
(SEE SIDEBAR)

2 TEASPOONS PERNOD

1 TABLESPOON TOMATO PASTE

SALT AND PEPPER, TO TASTE

1 LB. MONKFISH, CUBED

12 SMALL SHRIMP, SHELLED
AND DEVEINED

12 STEAMER CLAMS, RINSED

24 MUSSELS, RINSED
AND DEBEARDED

FRESH PARSLEY, FINELY CHOPPED,
FOR GARNISH

DIRECTIONS

1. Place 4 tablespoons of the olive oil in a saucepan and warm over medium heat. When the oil starts to shimmer, add the onion, leek, celery, and fennel and sauté until they are soft, about 10 minutes.

2. Add the garlic, thyme, bay leaf, orange zest, tomato, saffron, stocks, Pernod, and tomato paste. Season with salt and pepper and bring the stew to a boil. Reduce the heat to medium-low and simmer for 20 minutes.

3. Place the remaining oil in a skillet and warm it over medium heat. Season the fish and shrimp with salt and pepper. When the oil starts to shimmer, add the seafood to the pan and cook for 2 minutes on each side. Remove from the pan and set the seafood aside.

4. Add the clams to the broth and cook for 3 minutes. Add the mussels and cook for an additional 3 to 4 minutes. Discard any mussels that don't open. Add the fish and shrimp and cook until warmed through. Season with salt and pepper, ladle the soup warmed bowls, and garnish with parsley.

Saffron & Mussel Soup

INGREDIENTS

3 LBS. MUSSELS, RINSED AND DEBEARDED

3 CUPS WHITE WINE

4 TABLESPOONS UNSALTED BUTTER

2 LEEKS, TRIMMED, RINSED WELL, AND CHOPPED

2 CELERY STALKS, CHOPPED

¾ CUP CHOPPED FENNEL

1 CARROT, PEELED AND MINCED

2 GARLIC CLOVES, MINCED

⅛ TEASPOON SAFFRON

2 CUPS HEAVY CREAM

SALT AND PEPPER, TO TASTE

3 TOMATOES, CHOPPED

FRESH PARSLEY, FINELY CHOPPED, FOR GARNISH

MICROGREENS, FOR GARNISH

SHAVED RADISH, DRESSED WITH OLIVE OIL AND FRESH LEMON JUICE, FOR GARNISH

DIRECTIONS

1. Place the mussels and the wine in a large saucepan, cover, and cook over medium heat, shaking the pan occasionally, for 4 to 5 minutes, until the majority of the mussels have opened. Discard any unopened mussels. Drain, reserve the cooking liquid, and remove the meat from all but 18 of the mussels. Reserve the 18 mussels in their shells for garnish.

2. Add the butter to the saucepan and melt it over medium heat. Add the leeks, celery, fennel, carrot, and garlic and sauté until the vegetables start to soften, about 5 minutes.

3. Strain the reserved liquid through a fine sieve and add it to the saucepan. Cook for 10 minutes, until the liquid has reduced by one-quarter.

4. Add the saffron and the cream and bring the soup to a boil. Reduce the heat to low, season with salt and pepper, add the mussels and tomatoes, and cook gently until heated through.

5. Ladle the soup into warmed bowls and garnish with the parsley, microgreens, radish, and reserved mussels.

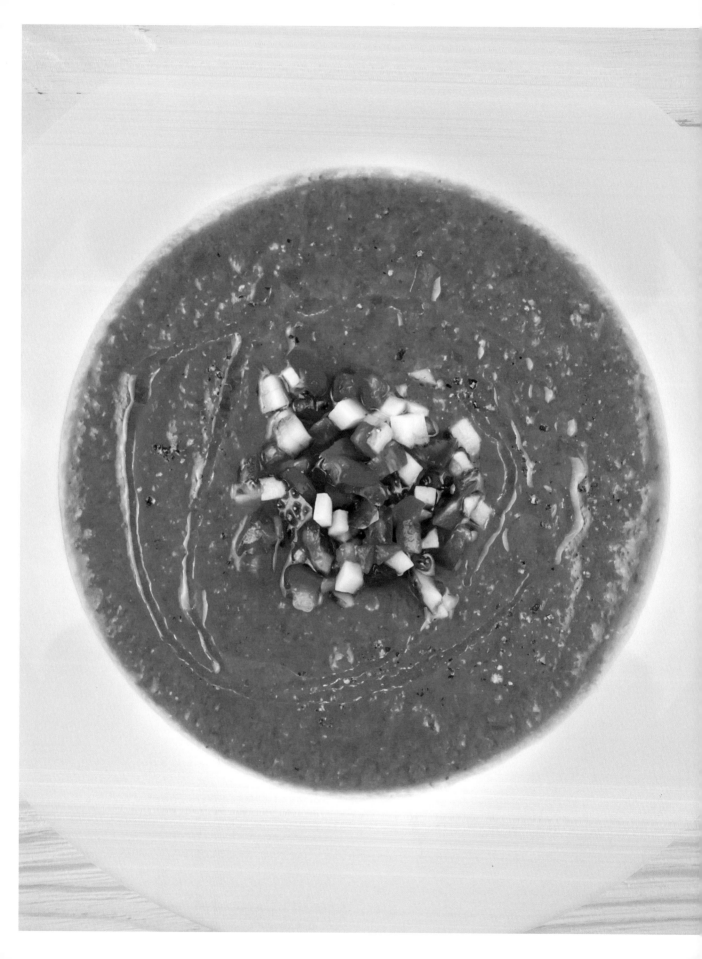

Gazpacho

INGREDIENTS

4 TOMATOES, CHOPPED, PLUS MORE FOR GARNISH

½ RED ONION, CHOPPED

½ CUCUMBER, CHOPPED, PLUS MORE FOR GARNISH

1 RED BELL PEPPER, STEMMED, SEEDS AND RIBS REMOVED, AND CHOPPED, PLUS MORE FOR GARNISH

1 CELERY STALK, CHOPPED

1 CUP CHOPPED DAY-OLD CRUSTY BREAD

2 TABLESPOONS FINELY CHOPPED FRESH PARSLEY

2 TABLESPOONS FINELY CHOPPED FRESH CHIVES

1 GARLIC CLOVE, MINCED

¼ CUP RED WINE VINEGAR

2 TABLESPOONS OLIVE OIL

1 TEASPOON FRESH LEMON JUICE

1 TEASPOON SUGAR

2 TEASPOONS TABASCO

1 TEASPOON WORCESTERSHIRE SAUCE

2 CUPS TOMATO JUICE

SALT AND PEPPER, TO TASTE

DIRECTIONS

1. Combine all of the ingredients in a large mixing bowl, cover, and place in the refrigerator to chill overnight.

2. Transfer the soup to a food processor and blitz until it reaches the desired consistency. Chill in the refrigerator for 1 hour. Taste, adjust the seasoning if necessary, ladle into chilled bowls, and garnish with additional chopped vegetables.

Eggplant & Zucchini Soup

YIELD: **4 SERVINGS**

ACTIVE TIME: **20 MINUTES**

TOTAL TIME: **1 HOUR AND 15 MINUTES**

INGREDIENTS

1 LARGE EGGPLANT, PEELED AND CHOPPED

2 ZUCCHINI, CHOPPED

1 ONION, CHOPPED

3 GARLIC CLOVES, MINCED

2 TABLESPOONS OLIVE OIL

3 CUPS VEGETABLE STOCK (SEE PAGE 103)

1 TABLESPOON FINELY CHOPPED FRESH OREGANO

1 TABLESPOON FINELY CHOPPED FRESH MINT, PLUS MORE FOR GARNISH

SALT AND PEPPER, TO TASTE

TZATZIKI (SEE PAGE 43), FOR SERVING

PITA BREAD (SEE PAGE 31), FOR SERVING

MINTY PICKLED CUCUMBERS (SEE PAGE 20), FOR SERVING

DIRECTIONS

1. Preheat oven to 425°F. Place the eggplant, zucchini, onion, and garlic in a baking dish, drizzle the olive oil over the mixture, and gently stir to coat. Place in the oven and roast for 30 minutes, removing to stir occasionally. Remove from the oven and let the vegetables cool briefly.

2. Place half of the roasted vegetables in a food processor. Add the stock and blitz until pureed. Place the puree in a medium saucepan, add the remaining roasted vegetables, and bring to a boil.

3. Stir in the oregano and mint and season with salt and pepper. Cook for 2 minutes and ladle into warmed bowls. Garnish with additional mint and serve with the Tzatziki, Pita Bread, and Minty Pickled Cucumbers.

Meatball & Orzo Soup

INGREDIENTS

FOR THE MEATBALLS

2 SLICES OF WHITE BREAD,
CRUSTS REMOVED, TORN INTO
SMALL PIECES

6 TABLESPOONS MILK

¾ LB. GROUND CHICKEN

½ ONION, CHOPPED

3 TABLESPOONS FINELY CHOPPED
FRESH PARSLEY

1 TABLESPOON ORANGE ZEST

2 GARLIC CLOVES, MINCED

1 EGG, BEATEN

SALT AND PEPPER, TO TASTE

2 TABLESPOONS OLIVE OIL

FOR THE SOUP

1 (14 OZ.) CAN OF CANNELLINI
BEANS, DRAINED AND RINSED

4 CUPS CHICKEN STOCK
(SEE PAGE 108)

Continued...

DIRECTIONS

1. To begin preparations for the meatballs, place the bread and milk in a bowl and let the mixture rest for 10 minutes.

2. Add the chicken, onion, parsley, orange zest, garlic, and egg and work the mixture with your hands until combined. Season with salt and pepper and form the mixture into 1-inch balls.

3. Place the oil in a large skillet and warm it over medium heat. When it starts to shimmer, add the meatballs and cook, turning them occasionally, until they are browned all over, about 10 minutes. Remove them from the pan with a slotted spoon and place them on a paper towel–lined plate to drain.

4. To begin preparations for the soup, place the cannellini beans and 1 cup of the stock in a food processor, puree until smooth, and set the mixture aside. Place the olive oil in a saucepan and warm over medium heat. When the oil starts to shimmer, add the onion, garlic, chili, celery, and carrot and cook until the vegetables start to soften, about 5 minutes.

5. Stir in the tomato paste, the cannellini puree, and the remaining stock and bring the soup to a boil. Reduce the heat so that the soup simmers and cook for 10 minutes.

6. Add the orzo and cook until it is tender, about 8 minutes. Add the meatballs, cook until cooked through, and then season with salt and pepper. Ladle the soup into warmed bowls and garnish with the Pecorino and basil.

2 TABLESPOONS OLIVE OIL

1 ONION, CHOPPED

1 GARLIC CLOVE, MINCED

1 BIRD'S EYE CHILI PEPPER,
STEMMED, SEEDS AND RIBS
REMOVED, AND CHOPPED

1 CELERY STALK, CHOPPED

1 CARROT, PEELED AND CHOPPED

1 TABLESPOON TOMATO PASTE

1½ CUPS ORZO

SALT AND PEPPER, TO TASTE

PECORINO CHEESE, GRATED,
FOR GARNISH

FRESH BASIL, FINELY CHOPPED,
FOR GARNISH

Italian Wedding Soup

YIELD: **4 SERVINGS**

ACTIVE TIME: **30 MINUTES**

TOTAL TIME: **1 HOUR AND 15 MINUTES**

INGREDIENTS

FOR THE MEATBALLS

¾ LB. GROUND CHICKEN

⅓ CUP PANKO

1 GARLIC CLOVE, MINCED

2 TABLESPOONS FINELY CHOPPED FRESH PARSLEY

¼ CUP GRATED PARMESAN CHEESE

1 TABLESPOON MILK

1 EGG, BEATEN

⅛ TEASPOON FENNEL SEEDS

⅛ TEASPOON RED PEPPER FLAKES

½ TEASPOON PAPRIKA

SALT AND PEPPER, TO TASTE

FOR THE SOUP

2 TABLESPOONS OLIVE OIL

1 ONION, CHOPPED

Continued...

DIRECTIONS

1. Preheat the oven to 350°F. To prepare the meatballs, place all of the ingredients in a mixing bowl and work the mixture with your hands until combined. Form the mixture into 1-inch balls and place them on a parchment-lined baking sheet. Place the meatballs in the oven and bake for 12 to 15 minutes, until browned and cooked through. Remove from the oven and set the meatballs aside.

2. To begin preparations for the soup, place the olive oil in a saucepan and warm over medium heat. When the oil starts to shimmer, add the onion, carrots, and celery and sauté until they start to soften, about 5 minutes.

3. Stir in the stock and the wine and bring the soup to a boil. Reduce the heat so that the soup simmers, add the pasta, and cook for 8 minutes.

4. Add the cooked meatballs and simmer for 5 minutes. Stir in the dill and the spinach and cook for 2 minutes, or until the spinach has wilted. Season with salt and pepper, ladle the soup into warmed bowls, and garnish with the Parmesan.

2 CARROTS, PEELED AND MINCED

1 CELERY STALK, MINCED

6 CUPS CHICKEN STOCK
(SEE PAGE 108)

¼ CUP WHITE WINE

½ CUP TUBETINI PASTA

2 TABLESPOONS FINELY CHOPPED
FRESH DILL

6 OZ. BABY SPINACH

SALT AND PEPPER, TO TASTE

PARMESAN CHEESE, GRATED,
FOR GARNISH

Tomato Soup with Chickpeas & Ditalini

YIELD: **4 SERVINGS**

ACTIVE TIME: **20 MINUTES**

TOTAL TIME: **45 MINUTES**

INGREDIENTS

2 TABLESPOONS OLIVE OIL

1 ONION, CHOPPED

2 GARLIC CLOVES, MINCED

2 (28 OZ.) CANS OF STEWED TOMATOES, PUREED

2 TABLESPOONS FINELY CHOPPED FRESH THYME

4 CUPS CHICKEN STOCK (SEE PAGE 108)

½ CUP DITALINI PASTA

1 (14 OZ.) CAN OF CHICKPEAS, DRAINED AND RINSED

¼ CUP FINELY CHOPPED FRESH PARSLEY

¼ CUP GRATED PARMESAN CHEESE, PLUS MORE FOR GARNISH

SALT AND PEPPER, TO TASTE

FRESH BASIL, FINELY CHOPPED, FOR GARNISH

DIRECTIONS

1. Place the olive oil in a large saucepan and warm over medium heat. When the oil starts to shimmer, add the onion and sauté until it starts to soften, about 5 minutes. Add the garlic, cook for 2 minutes, and stir in the pureed tomatoes, thyme, and stock.

2. Bring the soup to a boil, reduce the heat so that the soup simmers, and add the ditalini. Cook until the pasta is tender, 8 to 10 minutes.

3. Stir in the chickpeas, parsley, and Parmesan and cook for 3 minutes. Season with salt and pepper, ladle into warmed bowls, and garnish with additional Parmesan and the basil.

Broccoli & Anchovy Soup

INGREDIENTS

1 TABLESPOON OLIVE OIL

1 TABLESPOON UNSALTED BUTTER

1 ONION, CHOPPED

1 GARLIC CLOVE, MINCED

1½ CUPS CHOPPED PORTOBELLO
MUSHROOMS

1 BIRD'S EYE CHILI PEPPER,
STEMMED, SEEDS AND RIBS
REMOVED, AND CHOPPED

2 WHITE ANCHOVY FILLETS,
MINCED

1 CUP CHOPPED TOMATOES

¼ CUP WHITE WINE

4 CUPS VEGETABLE STOCK
(SEE PAGE 103)

2 CUPS BROCCOLI FLORETS

SALT AND PEPPER, TO TASTE

PARMESAN CHEESE, GRATED,
FOR GARNISH

DIRECTIONS

1. Place the olive oil and butter in a saucepan and warm over low heat. When the butter has melted, add the onion, garlic, mushrooms, chili, and anchovies and sauté until the onion starts to soften, about 5 minutes.

2. Stir in the tomatoes and the white wine and simmer, stirring occasionally, for 10 minutes.

3. Add the stock, raise the heat to medium-high, and bring the soup to a boil. Reduce the heat so that the soup simmers. Add the broccoli florets and cook for 10 minutes.

4. Season with salt and pepper, ladle into warmed bowls, and garnish with Parmesan cheese.

Great Northern Bean Soup with Panfried Artichoke & Prosciutto

YIELD: **4 SERVINGS**

ACTIVE TIME: **35 MINUTES**

TOTAL TIME: **1 HOUR**

INGREDIENTS

1 LARGE ARTICHOKE

OLIVE OIL, AS NEEDED

1 SMALL YELLOW ONION, DICED

2 GARLIC CLOVES, MINCED

1 (14 OZ.) CAN OF GREAT NORTHERN BEANS, DRAINED AND RINSED

4 CUPS CHICKEN STOCK (SEE PAGE 108)

4 SLICES OF PROSCIUTTO, TORN

SALT AND PEPPER, TO TASTE

2 TABLESPOONS FINELY CHOPPED FRESH PARSLEY

2 TEASPOONS FRESH LEMON JUICE

1 TEASPOON LEMON ZEST

DIRECTIONS

1. Bring water to a boil in a small saucepan and add the artichoke. Cover, reduce the heat to medium-low, and cook until the stem is just tender, about 10 minutes. Remove from the water and let cool.

2. Place a large saucepan over medium heat and add enough oil to coat the bottom. Add the onion to the pot and sauté until it just starts to soften, about 5 minutes. Add the garlic and sauté until it begins to brown, about 1 minute.

3. Add the beans and stock to the pot and cook for about 10 minutes. Then, puree the mixture using a blender or an immersion blender.

4. Place the prosciutto in a small pan and cook over medium heat until just starting to brown, about 5 minutes. Transfer to a plate and set aside.

5. When the artichoke is cool enough to handle, remove all of the leaves until you have just the core left. Carefully cut out the fibrous center, leaving the heart. Chop the heart into bite-sized pieces.

6. Coat the bottom of the pan that had the prosciutto in it with oil and warm over medium heat. Add the artichoke heart and cook, stirring occasionally, until browned on all sides, about 5 minutes. Transfer to the plate with the prosciutto.

7. Warm the white bean puree over medium heat and season with salt and pepper. Ladle into warmed bowls and divide the prosciutto, artichoke heart, chopped parsley, lemon juice, and lemon zest between them.

Asparagus & Pea Soup

INGREDIENTS

¾ LB. ASPARAGUS

2 TABLESPOONS UNSALTED BUTTER

1 LEEK, TRIMMED, RINSED WELL, AND CHOPPED

1¼ CUPS PEAS, ¼ CUP RESERVED FOR GARNISH

1 TABLESPOON FINELY CHOPPED FRESH PARSLEY

5 CUPS VEGETABLE STOCK (SEE PAGE 103)

½ CUP HEAVY CREAM

ZEST OF 2 LEMONS, HALF RESERVED FOR GARNISH

SALT AND PEPPER, TO TASTE

FRESH MINT LEAVES, FOR GARNISH

PARMESAN CHEESE, SHAVED, FOR GARNISH

DIRECTIONS

1. Remove the woody ends of the asparagus and discard. Separate the spears, remove the tips, set them aside, and chop what remains into 1-inch-long pieces.

2. Place the butter in a saucepan and melt over medium heat. Add the leek and sauté until it starts to soften, about 5 minutes.

3. Add the chopped asparagus, the cup of peas, and the parsley. Cook for 3 minutes, stir in the stock, and bring to a boil. Reduce the heat so that the soup simmers and cook until the vegetables are tender, 6 to 8 minutes.

4. Transfer the soup to a food processor, puree until smooth, and strain through a fine sieve.

5. Place the soup in a clean saucepan. Add the cream and lemon zest, season with salt and pepper, and bring to a simmer.

6. Bring a small pan of water to a boil and prepare an ice water bath. Add salt and the asparagus tips to the pan and cook for 3 to 4 minutes, or until tender. Remove the tips, submerge in the ice water bath, pat dry with paper towels, and set aside.

7. Ladle the soup into warmed bowls and garnish with the asparagus tips, reserved peas, mint leaves, reserved lemon zest, and Parmesan.

Smoked Chorizo & Cabbage Soup

YIELD: **4 SERVINGS**

ACTIVE TIME: **15 MINUTES**

TOTAL TIME: **30 MINUTES**

INGREDIENTS

2 TABLESPOONS OLIVE OIL

1 ONION, CHOPPED

¼ CUP FRESH THYME, CHOPPED

1 LB. DRIED SMOKED CHORIZO, SLICED INTO ¼-INCH PIECES

1 HEAD OF GREEN CABBAGE, CORED AND SLICED

1 TABLESPOON CUMIN SEEDS

1 CINNAMON STICK

6 CUPS CHICKEN STOCK (SEE PAGE 108)

SALT AND PEPPER, TO TASTE

DIRECTIONS

1. Place the olive oil in a medium saucepan and warm it over medium heat. When the oil starts to shimmer, add the onion and sauté until it starts to soften, about 5 minutes.

2. Add the thyme, chorizo, cabbage, cumin seeds, and cinnamon stick, cover the pan, and cook for 5 minutes, stirring occasionally.

3. Add the stock, raise the heat to high, and bring the soup to a boil. Reduce the heat so that the soup simmers and cook for an additional 10 minutes.

4. Season with salt and pepper and ladle into warmed bowls.

Leek & Seafood Stew

INGREDIENTS

2 TABLESPOONS OLIVE OIL

WHITE PARTS OF 2 LEEKS, TRIMMED, AND RINSED WELL, AND SLICED THIN

2 TEASPOONS CORIANDER SEEDS, CRUSHED

PINCH OF RED PEPPER FLAKES

3 CUPS LITTLE CREAMER POTATOES, SLICED THIN

1 (14 OZ.) CAN OF DICED TOMATOES, WITH THEIR LIQUID

4 CUPS FISH STOCK (SEE SIDEBAR)

1 CUP WHITE WINE

2 BAY LEAVES

1 STAR ANISE POD

ZEST OF 1 ORANGE

PINCH OF SAFFRON

1 LB. COD FILLETS, CUT INTO ½-INCH PIECES

1 LB. SMALL SQUID, BODIES HALVED AND SCORED, TENTACLES LEFT WHOLE

10 OZ. SHRIMP, SHELLED AND DEVEINED

SALT AND PEPPER, TO TASTE

DIRECTIONS

1. Place the olive oil in a medium saucepan and warm it over medium heat. When the oil starts to shimmer, add the leeks, crushed coriander seeds, and red pepper flakes and cook until the leeks start to soften, about 5 minutes.

2. Add the potatoes, tomatoes, stock, wine, bay leaves, star anise, orange zest, and saffron and bring the soup to a boil. Reduce the heat so that the soup simmers and cook until the potatoes are tender, about 15 minutes.

3. Add the cod and the squid to the soup and simmer until cooked through, 3 to 4 minutes. Add the shrimp and simmer until it is cooked through, about 2 minutes. Season the soup with salt and pepper and ladle it into warmed bowls.

FISH STOCK

Place ¼ cup olive oil in a stockpot and warm over low heat. Add 1 trimmed, rinsed, and chopped leek, 1 unpeeled, chopped onion, 2 chopped carrots, 1 chopped celery stalk and cook until the liquid they release has evaporated. Add ¾ lb. of whitefish bodies, 4 sprigs of fresh parsley, 3 sprigs of fresh thyme, 2 bay leaves, 1 teaspoon of black peppercorns and salt, and 8 cups water, raise the heat to high, and bring to a boil. Reduce heat so that the stock simmers and cook for 3 hours, while skimming to remove any impurities that float to the surface. Strain the stock through a fine sieve, let it cool slightly, and place in the refrigerator, uncovered, to chill. When the stock is completely cool, remove the fat layer from the top and cover. The stock will keep in the refrigerator for 3 to 5 days, and in the freezer for up to 3 months.

YIELD: **4 SERVINGS**

ACTIVE TIME: **20 MINUTES**

TOTAL TIME: **1 HOUR**

Rutabaga & Fig Soup

INGREDIENTS

2 TABLESPOONS OLIVE OIL

1 ONION, CHOPPED

4 CUPS PEELED AND CHOPPED
RUTABAGA

1 TABLESPOON HONEY

4 CUPS VEGETABLE STOCK
(SEE PAGE 103)

1 TEASPOON FINELY CHOPPED
FRESH THYME

16 BLACK MISSION FIGS

1 CUP BUTTERMILK

SALT AND PEPPER, TO TASTE

HONEYED FIGS (SEE PAGE 10),
FOR SERVING

SPICY CHICKPEAS (SEE PAGE 13),
FOR SERVING

DIRECTIONS

1. Place the olive oil in a medium saucepan and warm it over
    medium heat. When the oil starts to shimmer, add the onion
    and rutabaga and cook until the onion is soft, about 10
    minutes. Stir in the honey, stock, thyme, and figs and bring
    the soup to a boil.

2. Reduce the heat so that the soup simmers and cook until the
    rutabaga is tender, about 20 minutes.

3. Transfer the soup to a food processor or blender and puree
    until smooth. Return the soup to a clean pan, add the
    buttermilk, and bring to a simmer.

4. Season the soup with salt and pepper, ladle into warm bowls,
    and serve with the Honeyed Figs and BBQ Chickpeas.

Baby Spinach & Yogurt Soup

YIELD: **4 SERVINGS**

ACTIVE TIME: **20 MINUTES**

TOTAL TIME: **1 HOUR**

INGREDIENTS

½ CUP OLIVE OIL, PLUS 2
TABLESPOONS

1 ONION, CHOPPED

10 OZ. BABY SPINACH

2 SCALLIONS, TRIMMED
AND CHOPPED

¼ CUP LONG-GRAIN RICE

3½ CUPS VEGETABLE STOCK
(SEE PAGE 103)

1 GARLIC CLOVE, MINCED

1½ CUPS WHOLE-MILK YOGURT

2 TEASPOONS TURMERIC

SALT AND PEPPER, TO TASTE

DIRECTIONS

1. Place the 2 tablespoons of olive oil in a large saucepan and warm it over medium heat. When the oil starts to shimmer, add the onion and sauté until it starts to soften, about 5 minutes.

2. Add two-thirds of the spinach, cover the pan, and cook until the spinach is wilted, about 3 minutes.

3. Add the scallions, rice, and stock and simmer until the rice is tender, about 18 minutes.

4. Transfer the soup to a food processor or blender, add the garlic and remaining spinach, and puree until smooth. Strain through a fine sieve, return the soup to a clean pan, bring it to a simmer, and stir in the yogurt.

5. Place the remaining olive oil and the turmeric in a small bowl. Season with salt and pepper, stir to combine, and strain the oil through a fine sieve. Set the infused oil aside.

6. Season the soup with salt and pepper, ladle it into warm bowls, and top each portion with some of the infused oil.

Butternut Squash, Quinoa & Chicken Soup

YIELD: **4 SERVINGS**

ACTIVE TIME: **20 MINUTES**

TOTAL TIME: **1 HOUR AND 15 MINUTES**

INGREDIENTS

1 BUTTERNUT SQUASH, HALVED AND SEEDED

3 TABLESPOONS OLIVE OIL

2 CHICKEN BREASTS, CUT INTO ½-INCH CUBES

1 ONION, CHOPPED

2 GARLIC CLOVES, MINCED

4 CUPS CHICKEN STOCK (SEE PAGE 108)

1 (14 OZ.) CAN OF STEWED TOMATOES, DRAINED AND CHOPPED

1 TABLESPOON FINELY CHOPPED FRESH OREGANO

⅔ CUP QUINOA, RINSED

SALT AND PEPPER, TO TASTE

DIRECTIONS

1. Preheat the oven to 375°F. Place the butternut squash, cut side up, on a baking sheet, drizzle 2 tablespoons of the oil over it, and place it in the oven. Roast for 40 minutes, until the flesh is very tender. Remove from the oven and let cool.

2. Place the remaining oil in a Dutch oven and warm it over medium heat. When the oil starts to shimmer, add the chicken and cook, turning frequently, until it is evenly browned, about 8 minutes. Remove the chicken with a slotted spoon and set it aside.

3. Add the onion to the pot and cook until it has softened, about 5 minutes. Add the garlic, cook for 1 minute, and then add 3 cups of the stock, the stewed tomatoes, and the oregano. Bring to a boil and then reduce the heat so that the soup simmers.

4. Scoop the flesh of the butternut squash into a food processor or blender with the remaining stock. Puree until smooth.

5. Add the butternut squash puree, chicken, and quinoa to the simmering broth. Cook until the quinoa is tender, about 15 minutes. Season with salt and pepper and ladle into warmed bowls.

Spring Pea Soup with Lemon Ricotta

YIELD: **4 SERVINGS**

ACTIVE TIME: **15 MINUTES**

TOTAL TIME: **25 MINUTES**

INGREDIENTS

1 CUP RICOTTA CHEESE

¼ CUP HEAVY CREAM

2 TABLESPOONS LEMON ZEST

1 TABLESPOON KOSHER SALT, PLUS
2 TEASPOONS

12 CUPS WATER

6 STRIPS OF LEMON PEEL

3 CUPS PEAS

3 SHALLOTS, DICED

6 FRESH MINT LEAVES, PLUS MORE
FOR GARNISH

DIRECTIONS

1. Place the ricotta, cream, lemon zest, and the 2 teaspoons of salt in a food processor and blitz until combined. Season to taste and set the lemon ricotta aside.

2. Place the water and remaining salt in a saucepan and bring to a boil over medium heat. Add the strips of lemon peel to the saucepan with the peas and shallots. Cook for 2 to 3 minutes, until the peas are just cooked through. Drain, making sure to reserve 2 cups of the cooking liquid, and immediately transfer the peas, strips of lemon peel, and shallots to a blender. Add the mint leaves and half of the reserved cooking liquid, and puree until the desired consistency is achieved, adding more cooking liquid as needed.

3. Season to taste, ladle into warmed bowls, and place a spoonful of the lemon ricotta in each bowl. Garnish with additional mint and serve immediately, as the brilliant green color starts to fade as the soup cools.

Mediterranean Beef Stew

INGREDIENTS

1½ LBS. BEEF CHUCK, TRIMMED
AND CUT INTO 1-INCH PIECES

2 TABLESPOONS KOSHER SALT

1 TABLESPOON BLACK PEPPER

1 (14 OZ.) CAN OF DICED
TOMATOES, WITH THEIR LIQUID

1 CUP CHICKEN STOCK
(SEE PAGE 108)

6 GARLIC CLOVES, MINCED

6 CARROTS, PEELED AND CHOPPED

3 YELLOW ONIONS, MINCED

¼ CUP TOMATO PASTE

1 TABLESPOON HERBES DE
PROVENCE

2 TABLESPOONS WORCESTERSHIRE
SAUCE

3 CUPS RED WINE

¼ CUP SOY SAUCE

½ CUP KALAMATA OLIVES,
FOR GARNISH

DIRECTIONS

1. Place all of the ingredients, except for the olives, in a slow cooker and stir to combine. Cook on low until the beef is very tender, 6 to 8 hours.

2. Taste, adjust the seasoning as needed, ladle the stew into warmed bowls, and garnish with the olives.

Moroccan Lentil Stew

INGREDIENTS

1 CUP BROWN LENTILS

½ CUP GREEN LENTILS

4 CUPS VEGETABLE STOCK
(SEE PAGE 103)

3 CARROTS, PEELED AND CHOPPED

1 LARGE YELLOW ONION, PEELED
AND CHOPPED

3 GARLIC CLOVES, MINCED

3-INCH PIECE OF FRESH GINGER,
PEELED AND MINCED

ZEST AND JUICE OF 1 LEMON

3 TABLESPOONS SMOKED PAPRIKA

2 TABLESPOONS CINNAMON

1 TABLESPOON CORIANDER

1 TABLESPOON TURMERIC

1 TABLESPOON CUMIN

1½ TEASPOONS ALLSPICE

2 BAY LEAVES

SALT AND PEPPER, TO TASTE

1 (14 OZ.) CAN OF CANNELLINI
BEANS

FRESH MINT, FINELY CHOPPED,
FOR GARNISH

GOAT CHEESE, CRUMBLED,
FOR GARNISH

DIRECTIONS

1. Place the lentils in a fine sieve and rinse them to remove any impurities. Place all of the ingredients, save the cannellini beans and the garnishes, in a slow cooker. Cover and cook on low for 7½ hours.

2. After 7½ hours, stir in the cannellini beans. Cover and cook on low for 30 another minutes. Ladle into warmed bowls and garnish with fresh mint and goat cheese.

Vegetable Barley Soup

YIELD: **4 SERVINGS**

ACTIVE TIME: **20 MINUTES**

TOTAL TIME: **1 HOUR AND 30 MINUTES**

INGREDIENTS

2 TABLESPOONS OLIVE OIL

2 ONIONS, CHOPPED

2 CARROTS, PEELED AND CHOPPED

1 CUP PEARL BARLEY

3 TABLESPOONS TOMATO PASTE

1 TEASPOON TURMERIC

8 CUPS VEGETABLE STOCK
(SEE PAGE 103)

½ CUP PLAIN GREEK YOGURT

⅓ CUP FINELY CHOPPED
PARSLEY LEAVES

SALT AND PEPPER, TO TASTE

8 LIME WEDGES, FOR SERVING

DIRECTIONS

1. Place the olive oil in a large saucepan and warm it over medium heat. When the oil starts to shimmer, add the onions and sauté until they start to soften, about 5 minutes. Add the carrots, barley, tomato paste, and turmeric and cook for 2 minutes.

2. Add the stock and bring the soup to a boil. Reduce heat so that the soup simmers and cook until the barley is tender, about 1 hour.

3. Remove the soup from heat. Stir in the yogurt and parsley and season with salt and pepper. Ladle into warmed bowls and serve with the lime wedges.

YIELD: **4 SERVINGS**

ACTIVE TIME: **20 MINUTES**

TOTAL TIME: **45 MINUTES**

African Peanut & Quinoa Soup

INGREDIENTS

1 TABLESPOON OLIVE OIL

1 TABLESPOON UNSALTED BUTTER

1 RED ONION, CHOPPED

½ SWEET POTATO, PEELED
AND CHOPPED

1 GREEN BELL PEPPER,
STEMMED, SEEDS AND RIBS
REMOVED, AND CHOPPED

2 CELERY STALKS, CHOPPED

1 ZUCCHINI, CHOPPED

1 JALAPEÑO PEPPER,
STEMMED, SEEDS AND RIBS
REMOVED, AND MINCED

1 GARLIC CLOVE, MINCED

6 CUPS VEGETABLE STOCK
(SEE PAGE 103)

¾ CUP QUINOA, RINSED

1 TEASPOON CUMIN

½ CUP PEANUT BUTTER

SALT AND PEPPER, TO TASTE

FRESH OREGANO, FINELY
CHOPPED, FOR GARNISH

PEANUTS, TOASTED, FOR GARNISH

DIRECTIONS

1. Place the oil and butter in a large saucepan and warm over medium heat. When the butter has melted, add the red onion, sweet potato, bell pepper, celery, zucchini, jalapeño, and garlic and cook until the vegetables are soft, about 10 minutes.

2. Add the stock and bring the soup to a boil. Reduce the heat so that the soup simmers, stir in the quinoa and cumin, cover, and simmer until quinoa is tender, about 15 minutes.

3. Stir in the peanut butter and season the soup with salt and pepper. Ladle into warmed bowls and garnish with the oregano and toasted peanuts.

Vegetable Soup with Couscous

YIELD: **4 SERVINGS**

ACTIVE TIME: **15 MINUTES**

TOTAL TIME: **45 MINUTES**

INGREDIENTS

2 TABLESPOONS OLIVE OIL

1 ONION, CHOPPED

1 LARGE CARROT, PEELED AND CHOPPED

1 (14 OZ.) CAN OF DICED TOMATOES, DRAINED

5 GARLIC CLOVES, MINCED

6 CUPS VEGETABLE STOCK (SEE PAGE 103)

1¼ CUPS ISRAELI COUSCOUS

¼ TEASPOON CUMIN

¼ CUP FINELY CHOPPED FRESH CILANTRO

SALT AND PEPPER, TO TASTE

⅛ TEASPOON CAYENNE PEPPER

DIRECTIONS

1. Place the olive oil in a large saucepan and warm over medium heat. When the oil starts to shimmer, add the onion and carrot and sauté until they start to soften, about 5 minutes.

2. Stir in the remaining ingredients and bring the soup to a boil. Reduce the heat so that it simmers and cook until the couscous is tender, about 10 minutes. Ladle into warmed bowls.

Romesco de Peix

INGREDIENTS

½ CUP SLIVERED ALMONDS

½ TEASPOON SAFFRON

¼ CUP BOILING WATER

½ CUP OLIVE OIL

1 LARGE YELLOW ONION, CHOPPED

2 LARGE RED BELL PEPPERS, STEMMED, SEEDS AND RIBS REMOVED, AND CHOPPED

2½ TEASPOONS SWEET PAPRIKA

1 TABLESPOON SMOKED PAPRIKA

1 BAY LEAF

2 TABLESPOONS TOMATO PASTE

½ CUP SHERRY

2 CUPS FISH STOCK (SEE PAGE 141)

1 (28 OZ.) CAN OF CHOPPED TOMATOES, WITH THEIR LIQUID

SALT AND PEPPER, TO TASTE

1½ LBS. MONKFISH FILLETS, CHOPPED INTO LARGE PIECES

1 LB. MUSSELS, RINSED WELL AND DEBEARDED

FRESH CILANTRO, FINELY CHOPPED, FOR GARNISH

DIRECTIONS

1. Place the almonds in a large cast-iron skillet and toast them over medium heat until they are just browned. Transfer them to a food processor and pulse until they are finely ground. Place the saffron and boiling water in a bowl and let the mixture steep.

2. Place the olive oil in a Dutch oven and warm over medium heat. When it starts to shimmer, add the onion and bell peppers and sauté until the peppers are tender, about 15 minutes.

3. Add the sweet paprika, smoked paprika, bay leaf, and tomato paste and cook, stirring constantly, for 1 minute. Add the sherry and bring to a boil. Boil for 5 minutes and then stir in the stock, tomatoes, saffron, and the soaking liquid. Stir to combine, season with salt and pepper, and reduce the heat so that the mixture simmers.

4. Add the ground almonds and cook until the mixture thickens slightly, about 8 minutes. Add the fish and mussels, stir gently to incorporate, and simmer until the fish is cooked through and a majority of the mussels have opened, about 5 minutes. Discard any mussels that do not open.

5. Ladle the stew into warmed bowls and garnish with the cilantro.

YIELD: **4 SERVINGS**

ACTIVE TIME: **15 MINUTES**

TOTAL TIME: **30 MINUTES**

Avgolemono

INGREDIENTS

6 CUPS CHICKEN STOCK
(SEE PAGE 108)

½ CUP ORZO

3 EGGS

1 TABLESPOON FRESH
LEMON JUICE

1 TABLESPOON COLD WATER

1½ CUPS CHOPPED
LEFTOVER CHICKEN

SALT AND PEPPER, TO TASTE

LEMON SLICES, FOR GARNISH

FRESH PARSLEY, FINELY CHOPPED,
FOR GARNISH

DIRECTIONS

1. Place the stock in a large saucepan and bring it to a boil. Reduce heat so that the stock simmers. Add the orzo and cook until tender, about 5 minutes.

2. Strain the stock and orzo over a large bowl. Set the orzo aside. Return the stock to the pan and bring it to a simmer.

3. Place the eggs in a mixing bowl and beat until scrambled and frothy. Stir in the lemon juice and cold water. While stirring constantly, add approximately ½ cup of the stock to the mixture. Stir another cup of stock into the egg mixture and then stir the tempered eggs into the saucepan. Be careful not to let the stock come to boil once you add the egg mixture.

4. Add the chicken and return the orzo to the soup. Cook, while stirring, until everything is warmed through, about 5 minutes. Season with salt and pepper, ladle into warmed bowls, and garnish with the slices of lemon and the parsley.

CHAPTER 4

ENTREES

---

*Though the preceding chapters have plenty to offer,
the majority of your engagement and enjoyment of this style
of eating will center around the dishes collected here.*

*In keeping with the directives set down by the diet,
you'll find a much higher proportion of seafood dishes here than
there normally would be in a cookbook, a focus that is balanced out
by a shift away from the poultry dishes that become ubiquitous
in most diets, and an almost total avoidance of red meat.*

*Don't worry, though—there are dishes that will fit the bill
when you're in the mood for something rich and savory, including
a few that center around the lamb that carries a number
of feast-related dishes in the region.*

Lamb Kebabs

INGREDIENTS

2 LBS. BONELESS LEG OF LAMB, CUT INTO 1½-INCH CUBES

SALT AND PEPPER, TO TASTE

3 TABLESPOONS OLIVE OIL

1½ CUP RED WINE

4 GARLIC CLOVES, CRUSHED

1 SHALLOT, MINCED

2 TEASPOONS FINELY CHOPPED FRESH ROSEMARY

1 TEASPOON CUMIN

2 RED ONIONS, CHOPPED

2 RED BELL PEPPERS, STEMMED, SEEDS AND RIBS REMOVED, AND CHOPPED

BAMIES (SEE PAGE 94), FOR SERVING

DIRECTIONS

1. Place all of the ingredients, except for the red onions, peppers, and Bamies, in a mixing bowl or large resealable plastic bag. Toss to combine, place the bag in the refrigerator, and marinate for 4 hours, shaking or stirring occasionally. If time allows, you can marinate the lamb overnight.

2. Remove the bag from the refrigerator about 1 hour before you are going to start grilling. Transfer the lamb to a platter and let rest at room temperature. If using bamboo skewers, soak them in water.

3. Preheat your gas or charcoal grill to medium-high heat (450°F) and begin assembling the skewers. Place approximately 4 pieces of lamb on each skewer, making sure to align the pieces of onion and pepper in between each piece of lamb.

4. Place the skewers on the grill and cook, while turning, until the lamb is medium-rare and browned all over, about 10 to 12 minutes. Transfer the kebabs to a large cutting board and let them rest for 5 minutes before serving with the Bamies.

Lemon & Rosemary Chicken with Roasted Vegetables

YIELD: **4 SERVINGS**

ACTIVE TIME: **25 MINUTES**

TOTAL TIME: **1 HOUR**

INGREDIENTS

2 EGGPLANTS, CHOPPED

3 BELL PEPPERS, STEMMED, SEEDS AND RIBS REMOVED, AND SLICED

2 ZUCCHINI, SLICED

2 CUPS CHERRY TOMATOES

1 ONION, CHOPPED

3 GARLIC CLOVES, MINCED

¼ CUP OLIVE OIL

SALT AND PEPPER, TO TASTE

4 BONELESS, SKINLESS CHICKEN BREASTS

2 TABLESPOONS FRESH LEMON JUICE

4 SPRIGS OF FRESH ROSEMARY

DIRECTIONS

1. Preheat the oven to 400°F. Place all of the vegetables in a baking dish, drizzle 2 tablespoons of the olive oil over the top, and season them with salt and pepper. Place the vegetables in the oven and roast until the zucchini is just tender, about 30 minutes. Remove from the oven and set aside. Leave the oven on.

2. While the vegetables are roasting, place the chicken breasts in a mixing bowl, season them with salt and pepper, and add the lemon juice. Toss until the chicken is coated and let them rest at room temperature.

3. Place the remaining olive oil in a large skillet and warm over medium-high heat. When the oil starts to shimmer, add the chicken breasts and cook until browned, about 4 minutes. Turn the chicken breasts over, add the rosemary to the pan, and begin basting the chicken breasts with the oil. Cook until browned on the other side, remove the pan from heat, and continue to baste the chicken with the rosemary-infused oil.

4. Place the chicken breasts on the vegetables, drizzle any remaining infused oil over them, and place them in the oven. Bake until the chicken breasts are cooked through, about 10 minutes. Remove from the oven and let them rest briefly before serving.

YIELD: **4 SERVINGS**

ACTIVE TIME: **30 MINUTES**

TOTAL TIME: **1 HOUR AND 45 MINUTES**

Tagine with Prunes

INGREDIENTS

3 LBS. BONE-IN, SKIN-ON
CHICKEN THIGHS

SALT AND PEPPER, TO TASTE

2 TABLESPOONS OLIVE OIL,
PLUS MORE AS NEEDED

5 GARLIC CLOVES, MINCED

1¼ TEASPOONS SWEET PAPRIKA

½ TEASPOON CUMIN

¼ TEASPOON GROUND GINGER

¼ TEASPOON CORIANDER

¼ TEASPOON CINNAMON

¼ TEASPOON CAYENNE PEPPER

1 TABLESPOON LEMON ZEST

2 TABLESPOONS HONEY

1 LARGE ONION, SLICED

2 CARROTS, PEELED AND SLICED

2 CUPS CHICKEN STOCK
(SEE PAGE 108)

2 TABLESPOONS FINELY
CHOPPED FRESH PARSLEY,
PLUS MORE FOR GARNISH

1 CUP PRUNES

3 TABLESPOONS FRESH
LEMON JUICE

DIRECTIONS

1. Pat the chicken dry and season it with salt and pepper. Place the oil in a Dutch oven and warm it over medium-high heat. When the oil starts to shimmer, add the chicken in two batches, cooking until brown on each side, about 10 minutes. Transfer the chicken to a plate.

2. Remove all but 1 tablespoon of the oil and rendered fat from the pot. Add all of the remaining ingredients, except for the prunes and lemon juice, and cook until the carrots start to soften, about 8 minutes.

3. Return the chicken to the pot, bring it to a simmer, and then cover the Dutch oven. Reduce the heat to medium-low and simmer the tagine until the chicken is cooked through and tender, about 1 hour.

4. Stir in the prunes and lemon juice, season the tagine with salt and pepper, and serve, garnishing each portion with additional parsley.

DUKKAH

Place a large, dry cast-iron skillet over medium heat and add 2 tablespoons of pumpkin seeds, pistachios, peanuts, and thyme leaves, 1 teaspoon of black peppercorns, dried mint, coriander seeds, and cumin seeds, and 1 tablespoon sesame seeds. Toast, while stirring continuously, until the seeds and nuts are lightly browned. Remove the mixture from the pan and use a mortar and pestle or a spice grinder to grind it into a powder. Stir in 2 teaspoons of kosher salt and use as desired.

Halibut with Dukkah

YIELD: **4 SERVINGS**

ACTIVE TIME: **10 MINUTES**

TOTAL TIME: **40 MINUTES**

INGREDIENTS

1½ LBS. HALIBUT FILLETS

2 TABLESPOONS DUKKAH
(SEE SIDEBAR)

1 TABLESPOON OLIVE OIL

1 CUP PLAIN GREEK YOGURT

1 PINCH OF DRIED MINT

¼ CUP COCONUT OIL

1 (12 OZ.) PACKAGE OF
FROZEN SPINACH

LEMON WEDGES, FOR SERVING

DIRECTIONS

1. Pat the halibut fillets dry with a paper towel. Place them on a plate and coat with a thick layer of the Dukkah. Let them stand at room temperature for 15 minutes.

2. Place the olive oil, yogurt, and mint in a bowl and stir to combine. Set the mixture aside.

3. Place a large cast-iron skillet over medium heat and add the coconut oil. When the oil starts to shimmer, add the halibut and cook, while turning over once, until browned and cooked through, about 3 minutes per side.

4. Use a thin spatula to remove the fish from the pan and set it aside. Add the spinach and sauté until thawed and cooked through, about 10 minutes.

5. Serve the fish with the spinach, a dollop of the mint-and-yogurt sauce, the lemon wedges, and any remaining Dukkah.

Pesto Chicken with Charred Tomatoes

INGREDIENTS

2 LBS. CHICKEN PIECES

SALT AND PEPPER, TO TASTE

2 BATCHES OF BASIL PESTO
(SEE SIDEBAR)

4 PLUM TOMATOES, HALVED

DIRECTIONS

1. Season the chicken with salt and pepper. Place the pesto in a bowl, add the chicken pieces, and stir until they are evenly coated. Cover the bowl and let the chicken marinate in the refrigerator for 2 hours.

2. Preheat the oven to 400°F. Remove the chicken from the refrigerator and let it come to room temperature.

3. Place the chicken in a baking dish. Season the tomatoes with salt and pepper and place them in the baking dish. Cover the dish with foil, place it in the oven, and roast for 25 minutes. Remove the foil and continue roasting until the chicken is cooked through, about 25 minutes. Remove from the oven and let the chicken rest for 10 minutes before serving.

BASIL PESTO

Warm a small skillet over low heat for 1 minute. Add ¼ cup walnuts and cook, while stirring, until they begin to give off a toasty aroma, 2 to 3 minutes. Transfer to a plate and let the walnuts cool completely. Place 3 garlic cloves and the walnuts in a food processor or blender and pulse until the mixture is a coarse meal. Season with salt, add 2 firmly packed cups of fresh basil leaves, and pulse until finely minced. Transfer the mixture to a medium bowl and add ½ cup olive oil in a thin stream as you quickly whisk it in. Stir in ¼ cup of grated Parmesan cheese and ¼ cup of grated Pecorino Sardo cheese and stir until thoroughly incorporated. Season to taste and use as desired. The pesto will keep in the refrigerator for up to 4 days and in the freezer for up to 3 months.

Braised Chicken with Polenta

YIELD: **4 SERVINGS**

ACTIVE TIME: **15 MINUTES**

TOTAL TIME: **1 HOUR AND 30 MINUTES**

INGREDIENTS

2 LBS. CHICKEN THIGHS, CHOPPED

SALT AND PEPPER, TO TASTE

2 TABLESPOONS OLIVE OIL

3 CUPS CHICKEN STOCK
(SEE PAGE 108)

½ CUP PITTED GREEN OLIVES

½ CUP SUN-DRIED TOMATOES IN
OLIVE OIL, DRAINED

½ CUP CHOPPED PORTOBELLO
MUSHROOMS

2 CUPS MEDIUM-GRAIN CORNMEAL

2 CUPS WATER

3 TABLESPOONS UNSALTED BUTTER

FRESH PARSLEY, FINELY CHOPPED,
FOR GARNISH

DIRECTIONS

1. Preheat the oven to 325°F. Season the chicken thighs with salt and pepper. Place the olive oil in a Dutch oven and warm it over medium-high heat. When the oil starts to shimmer, add the chicken thighs and cook until browned on both sides, about 4 minutes per side. Add 1 cup of the stock, the olives, tomatoes, and mushrooms, cover the Dutch oven, and place it in the oven. Cook until the chicken thighs are very tender, about 1 hour.

2. While the chicken thighs are in the oven, place the cornmeal, water, and the remaining stock in a large saucepan. Bring to a boil over medium-high heat, reduce the heat so that the mixture simmers, and cook, stirring frequently, until the mixture is creamy, about 45 minutes.

3. Stir the butter into the polenta and ladle it into warmed bowls. Top with the chicken and vegetables and garnish with parsley.

Mediterranean Wraps

INGREDIENTS

4 BONELESS, SKINLESS
CHICKEN BREASTS

SALT AND PEPPER, TO TASTE

2 TABLESPOONS OLIVE OIL

4 PIECES OF PITA BREAD
(SEE PAGE 31)

½ CUP PLAIN GREEK YOGURT

1 CUP CRUMBLED FETA CHEESE

½ CUP CHOPPED ROASTED
RED PEPPERS

½ CUP KALAMATA OLIVES,
PITTED AND CHOPPED

½ ONION, CHOPPED

½ CUP CHOPPED LETTUCE

2 TABLESPOONS FRESH
LEMON JUICE

DIRECTIONS

1. Season the chicken breasts with salt and pepper. Place the olive oil in a large skillet and warm over medium-high heat. When the oil starts to shimmer, add the chicken breasts and cook until they are browned all over and cooked through, about 5 minutes per side. Remove the chicken breasts from the pan and let them cool. When cool enough to handle, shred them with a fork.

2. Working with one pita at a time, place them in the skillet, set the heat to medium, and cook them until warmed and browned on each side, about 1 minute per side. Place the pitas on the serving plates, spread the yogurt in the center of each one, and then pile the chicken, feta, roasted red peppers, olives, onion, and lettuce on top.

3. Sprinkle the lemon juice over the mixture, roll the pitas up tightly, and serve.

YIELD: **4 SERVINGS**

ACTIVE TIME: **1 HOUR AND 15 MINUTES**

TOTAL TIME: **2 HOURS**

Moussaka

INGREDIENTS

FOR THE FILLING

4 CUPS COLD WATER

¼ CUP KOSHER SALT, PLUS MORE
TO TASTE

1 LARGE EGGPLANT, TRIMMED
AND SLICED

5 TABLESPOONS OLIVE OIL

1 LB. GROUND LAMB

1 ONION, DICED

3 GARLIC CLOVES, MINCED

½ CUP DRY RED WINE

1 CUP TOMATO SAUCE

2 TABLESPOONS FINELY CHOPPED
FRESH PARSLEY

1 TEASPOON DRIED OREGANO

½ TEASPOON CINNAMON

BLACK PEPPER, TO TASTE

Continued...

DIRECTIONS

1. Preheat the oven to 350°F. To begin preparations for the filling, place the cold water in a bowl, add the salt, and stir. When the salt has dissolved, add the eggplant and let it soak for about 20 minutes. Drain the eggplant and rinse with cold water. Squeeze to remove as much water as you can, place it on a pile of paper towels, and pat dry. Set aside.

2. While the eggplant is soaking, add a tablespoon of the olive oil to a large cast-iron skillet and warm it over medium-high heat. When the oil starts to shimmer, add the ground lamb and cook, using a fork to break it up, until it is browned, about 8 minutes. Transfer the cooked lamb to a bowl and set it aside.

3. Add 2 tablespoons of the olive oil and the eggplant to the skillet and cook, stirring frequently until it starts to brown, about 5 minutes. Transfer the cooked eggplant to the bowl containing the lamb and add the rest of the oil, the onion, and the garlic to the skillet. Sauté until the onion is translucent, about 3 minutes, return the lamb and eggplant to the skillet, and stir in the wine, tomato sauce, parsley, oregano, and cinnamon. Reduce the heat to low and simmer for about 15 minutes, stirring occasionally. Season with salt and pepper and remove the pan from heat.

4. To begin preparations for the crust, place the eggs in a large bowl and beat them lightly. Place a saucepan over medium heat and melt the butter. Reduce the heat to medium-low and add the flour. Stir constantly until the mixture is smooth.

Continued...

FOR THE CRUST

5 EGGS

6 TABLESPOONS UNSALTED BUTTER

⅓ CUP ALL-PURPOSE FLOUR

2½ CUPS MILK

⅔ CUP GRATED PARMESAN CHEESE

⅓ CUP FRESH DILL OR PARSLEY, CHOPPED

5. While stirring constantly, gradually add the milk and bring the mixture to a boil. When the mixture reaches a boil, remove the pan from heat. Gradually stir approximately half of the mixture in the saucepan into the beaten eggs. Stir the tempered eggs into the saucepan and then add the cheese and dill or parsley. Stir to combine and pour the mixture over the lamb mixture in the skillet, using a rubber spatula to smooth the top.

6. Place the skillet in the oven and bake until the crust is set and golden brown, about 35 minutes. Remove from the oven and let the moussaka rest for 5 minutes before serving.

Tarhana with Green Beans & Tomatoes

YIELD: **4 SERVINGS**

ACTIVE TIME: **30 MINUTES**

TOTAL TIME: **1 HOUR**

INGREDIENTS

6 PLUM TOMATOES

3 TABLESPOONS OLIVE OIL

1 ONION, MINCED

¼ TEASPOON KOSHER SALT, PLUS MORE TO TASTE

1 GARLIC CLOVE, MINCED

1½ LBS. FRESH GREEN BEANS, TRIMMED

1½ CUPS CHICKEN OR VEGETABLE STOCK (SEE PAGES 108 OR 103, RESPECTIVELY), PLUS MORE AS NEEDED

⅔ CUP TARHANA

¼ CUP FRESH BASIL LEAVES, SHREDDED

BLACK PEPPER, TO TASTE

DIRECTIONS

1. Bring a medium saucepan of water to a boil. Add the tomatoes and boil for 1 minute. Use tongs to transfer them to a cutting board and let them cool. When cool enough to handle, peel the tomatoes and discard the skins. Cut the flesh into quarters, remove the seeds and discard them, and mince the flesh.

2. Warm a large, deep skillet over medium-low heat for 2 to 3 minutes. Add the olive oil and raise the heat to medium. When it begins to shimmer, add the onion and a couple pinches of salt and cook, stirring occasionally, until the onion begins to gently sizzle. Reduce the heat to low, cover, and cook until the onion is very soft, about 15 minutes. Add the garlic and cook, stirring continuously, for 1 minute. Stir in the tomatoes and a couple pinches of salt and raise the heat to medium-high. Once the sauce begins to bubble, reduce the heat to low, cover the pan, and cook, stirring occasionally, until the tomatoes start to collapse, about 10 minutes.

3. Add the green beans, stock, the ¼ teaspoon of salt, and the tarhana. Raise the heat to medium-high and bring the mixture to a gentle simmer. Reduce heat to medium-low and cook, stirring occasionally, until the green beans and tarhana are tender, 15 to 20 minutes. Add more stock as necessary.

4. Season to taste, remove the pan from heat, and stir in the basil and black pepper. You can serve this hot or at room temperature.

Baked Cod with Lemons, Capers & Leeks

YIELD: **4 SERVINGS**

ACTIVE TIME: **15 MINUTES**

TOTAL TIME: **1 HOUR**

INGREDIENTS

½ LB. LEEKS, TRIMMED AND RINSED WELL

2 TABLESPOONS OLIVE OIL

SALT AND PEPPER, TO TASTE

1½ LBS. COD FILLETS

2 TABLESPOONS FRESH LEMON JUICE

3 TABLESPOONS CAPERS

½ LEMON, SLICED THIN

LEMON WEDGES, FOR SERVING

DIRECTIONS

1. Preheat the oven to 400°F. Pat the leeks dry, place them in a baking dish, drizzle the olive oil over them, and season with salt and pepper. Place the leeks in the oven and roast until they start to brown, about 25 minutes.

2. Remove the leeks from the oven, place the cod fillets on top of them, and sprinkle the lemon juice over the fish. Distribute the capers and slices of lemon over the cod fillets and place the baking dish back in the oven. Roast until the cod is cooked through and can be flaked with a fork, about 25 minutes. Serve with lemon wedges on the side.

Orange Chicken with Roasted Vegetables & Olives

YIELD: **4 SERVINGS**

ACTIVE TIME: **30 MINUTES**

TOTAL TIME: **1 HOUR**

INGREDIENTS

3 CARROTS, PEELED AND CHOPPED

1 SMALL FENNEL BULB, TRIMMED, CORED, AND SLICED THIN

1 CUP CHERRY TOMATOES

¼ CUP OLIVE OIL

4 GARLIC CLOVES, MINCED

2 TEASPOONS FINELY CHOPPED FRESH ROSEMARY

2 TEASPOONS ORANGE ZEST

1 TABLESPOON RED WINE VINEGAR

SALT AND PEPPER, TO TASTE

2 LBS. BONELESS, SKINLESS CHICKEN BREASTS

JUICE OF 2 ORANGES

¼ CUP PITTED KALAMATA OLIVES, CHOPPED, FOR GARNISH

FRESH BASIL, FINELY CHOPPED, FOR GARNISH

DIRECTIONS

1. Preheat the oven to 400°F. Place the carrots, fennel, tomatoes, 2 tablespoons of the oil, the garlic, rosemary, orange zest, and red wine vinegar in a bowl, season the mixture with salt and pepper, and stir to combine.

2. Transfer the vegetable mixture to a baking dish, place it in the oven, and roast until the vegetables are almost completely tender, about 40 minutes. Remove the dish from the oven and set it aside. Leave the oven on.

3. While the vegetables are roasting, season the chicken with salt and pepper, place it in a bowl, and add the orange juice. Stir until the chicken is coated and let the mixture marinate.

4. Place the remaining olive oil in a skillet and warm it over medium-high heat. When the oil starts to shimmer, add the chicken and cook until browned on both sides, about 6 minutes. Remove the chicken from the pan and place it on top of the vegetable mixture in the baking dish.

5. Place the baking dish in the oven and roast until the chicken is cooked all the way through, about 16 minutes.

6. Divide the vegetables between the serving dishes, top each portion with a chicken breast, and sprinkle the olives and basil over each dish.

Stuffed Eggplants

INGREDIENTS

2 LARGE EGGPLANTS, HALVED

2 TABLESPOONS OLIVE OIL, PLUS MORE AS NEEDED

½ CUP QUINOA, RINSED

1 CUP WATER

2 ONIONS, CHOPPED

3 GARLIC CLOVES, MINCED

2 BELL PEPPERS, STEMMED, SEEDS AND RIBS REMOVED, AND CHOPPED

1 LB. GROUND LAMB

SALT AND PEPPER, TO TASTE

½ TEASPOON GARAM MASALA

2 TEASPOONS CUMIN

FRESH PARSLEY, FINELY CHOPPED, FOR GARNISH

DIRECTIONS

1. Preheat the oven to 400°F. Place the eggplants on a baking sheet, drizzle olive oil over the top, and place them in the oven. Roast until the flesh is tender, about 30 minutes. Remove from the oven and let the eggplants cool slightly. When cool enough to handle, scoop out the flesh, mince it, and place it in a mixing bowl. Set the hollowed-out eggplants aside and leave the oven on.

2. Place the quinoa and water in a saucepan and bring to a boil over medium heat. Let the quinoa boil until it has absorbed all of the water. Remove the pan from heat, cover it, and let it steam for 5 minutes. Fluff with a fork and let cool slightly.

3. Place the olive oil in a large skillet and warm it over medium-high heat. When the oil starts to shimmer, add the onions, garlic, and bell peppers and sauté until the onions and peppers start to soften, about 5 minutes. Add the ground lamb, season it with salt and pepper, stir in the garam masala and cumin, and cook, breaking the lamb up with a fork, until it is browned, about 6 minutes. Transfer the mixture to the bowl containing the minced eggplant. Add the quinoa to the bowl and stir until the mixture is combined.

4. Fill the cavities of the hollowed-out eggplants with the lamb-and-quinoa mixture. Place them on a baking sheet, place them in the oven, and roast until they are starting to collapse, about 15 minutes. Remove from the oven and let them cool slightly before garnishing with the parsley.

Mediterranean Turkey Burgers

YIELD: **4 SERVINGS**

ACTIVE TIME: **15 MINUTES**

TOTAL TIME: **40 MINUTES**

INGREDIENTS

¼ CUP OLIVE OIL

2 SHALLOTS, CHOPPED

3 GARLIC CLOVES, MINCED

1 LARGE EGG

2 TABLESPOONS WHOLE MILK

½ CUP ITALIAN BREAD CRUMBS

¼ CUP CHOPPED OIL-CURED BLACK OLIVES

½ CUP SUN-DRIED TOMATOES IN OLIVE OIL, DRAINED AND CHOPPED

¼ CUP GRATED PARMESAN CHEESE

2 TABLESPOONS FINELY CHOPPED FRESH PARSLEY

1 TABLESPOON FINELY CHOPPED FRESH OREGANO

1¼ LBS. GROUND TURKEY

Continued...

DIRECTIONS

1. Place half of the olive oil in a small skillet and warm it over medium-high heat. When the oil starts to shimmer, add the shallots and garlic and sauté until the shallots are translucent, about 3 minutes. Remove the pan from heat and set it aside.

2. Place the egg and milk in a mixing bowl, stir to combine, and then stir in the bread crumbs, olives, tomatoes, cheese, parsley, and oregano. Add the turkey and the shallot mixture, season with salt and pepper, and stir until thoroughly combined. Working with wet hands, form the mixture into four patties.

3. Place the yogurt, lemon juice, and sumac powder in a bowl, stir to combine, and set the mixture aside.

4. Place the remaining oil in a large skillet and warm it over medium heat. When the oil starts to shimmer, add the burger patties and cook until browned and cooked through, about 6 minutes per side. Depending on the thickness of the patties, you may want to cover the skillet to ensure that they are cooked through.

5. Serve the burgers with the sumac yogurt, hamburger buns (if desired), cucumber, lettuce, and Horiatiki Salad.

SALT AND PEPPER, TO TASTE

½ CUP GREEK YOGURT

1 TEASPOON FRESH LEMON JUICE

1 TABLESPOON SUMAC POWDER

WHOLE WHEAT HAMBURGER BUNS,
FOR SERVING (OPTIONAL)

1 CUCUMBER, SLICED THIN,
FOR SERVING

LETTUCE LEAVES, FOR SERVING

HORIATIKI SALAD (SEE PAGE 53),
FOR SERVING

YIELD: **4 SERVINGS**

ACTIVE TIME: **5 MINUTES**

TOTAL TIME: **10 MINUTES**

Lemon & Garlic Shrimp

INGREDIENTS

2 TABLESPOONS OLIVE OIL

1 LB. SHRIMP, SHELLED AND DEVEINED

8 GARLIC CLOVES, MINCED

½ TEASPOON LEMON-PEPPER SEASONING

1½ TABLESPOONS FRESH LEMON JUICE

1 TABLESPOON FINELY CHOPPED FRESH PARSLEY, FOR GARNISH

DIRECTIONS

1. Place the olive oil in a large skillet and warm it over medium heat. When the oil starts to shimmer, add the shrimp and cook, without stirring, for 3 minutes. Remove the shrimp from the pan with a slotted spoon and set them aside.

2. Reduce the heat to medium-low and add the garlic and lemon-pepper seasoning. Cook until the garlic has softened, about 3 minutes. Return the shrimp to the pan and cook until warmed through, about 1 minute. To serve, sprinkle the lemon juice over the shrimp and garnish with the parsley.

YIELD: **4 SERVINGS**

ACTIVE TIME: **40 MINUTES**

TOTAL TIME: **2 HOURS**

Briam

INGREDIENTS

3 YUKON GOLD POTATOES,
PEELED AND SLICED THIN

3 ZUCCHINI, SLICED THIN

SALT AND PEPPER, TO TASTE

1 TABLESPOON FINELY CHOPPED
FRESH OREGANO

2 TEASPOONS FINELY CHOPPED
FRESH ROSEMARY

½ CUP FRESH PARSLEY,
FINELY CHOPPED

4 GARLIC CLOVES, MINCED

3 TABLESPOONS OLIVE OIL

4 TOMATOES, SEEDED
AND CHOPPED

1 LARGE RED ONION, HALVED
AND SLICED THIN

DIRECTIONS

1. Preheat the oven to 400°F. Place the potatoes and zucchini
    in a bowl, season with salt and pepper, and then add the
    oregano, rosemary, parsley, garlic, and olive oil. Stir until the
    vegetables are evenly coated and set aside.

2. Cover the bottom of a baking dish with half of the tomatoes.
    Arrange the potatoes, zucchini, and onion in rows, working
    in from the edge of the dish to the center and alternating the
    vegetables as you go. Top with the remaining tomatoes and
    cover with foil.

3. Place the dish in the oven and roast for 45 minutes.
    Remove from the oven, remove the foil, and roast for another
    40 minutes, until the vegetables are charred and tender.
    Remove from the oven and let cool briefly before serving.

Braised Lamb with Minty Peas

INGREDIENTS

2 TABLESPOONS OLIVE OIL

1 YELLOW ONION, CHOPPED

2 LBS. BONELESS LAMB SHOULDER, CUT INTO 1-INCH CHUNKS

SALT AND PEPPER, TO TASTE

½ CUP HONEY

1 GARLIC CLOVE, MINCED

1 TEASPOON CORIANDER

½ TEASPOON CUMIN, OPTIONAL

¼ TEASPOON CAYENNE PEPPER, OR TO TASTE

1 TEASPOON GROUND CARAWAY SEED

½ TEASPOON GROUND FENNEL

1 CUP BEEF STOCK (SEE PAGE 111)

3 SPRIGS OF FRESH MINT

3 CUPS PEAS

1 CUP SLIVERED ALMONDS

FRESH LEMON JUICE, TO TASTE

DIRECTIONS

1. Place the olive oil in a large, deep skillet and warm it over medium heat. When the oil starts to shimmer, add the onion and sauté until it is soft, about 10 minutes. Remove with a slotted spoon and raise heat to medium-high. Add the lamb, season with salt and pepper, and cook, turning frequently, until the pieces are browned all over.

2. Turn off the heat and let the pan cool slightly. Set the heat to medium and add the honey. Cook, stirring, until honey has thinned and the lamb is coated. Stir in the garlic, add the seasonings and stock, and return the onions to the pan. Cover the pan and simmer until the lamb is very tender, about 1 hour.

3. When the lamb is close to ready, place the sprigs of mint and peas in a saucepan and cover with water. Cook over medium heat until the peas are tender, approximately 4 minutes for fresh peas and 7 minutes if using frozen. Drain, discard the mint, and cover the pan to keep warm.

4. Taste the lamb and adjust the seasoning as necessary. Stir in the almonds and lemon juice and serve with the peas.

Mediterranean Chicken Bake

YIELD: **6 SERVINGS**

ACTIVE TIME: **15 MINUTES**

TOTAL TIME: **45 MINUTES**

INGREDIENTS

2 LBS. BONELESS, SKINLESS CHICKEN BREASTS, HALVED ALONG THEIR EQUATORS

SALT AND PEPPER, TO TASTE

1 TABLESPOON FINELY CHOPPED FRESH OREGANO

1 TEASPOON FINELY CHOPPED FRESH THYME

1 TEASPOON PAPRIKA

4 GARLIC CLOVES, MINCED

3 TABLESPOONS OLIVE OIL, PLUS MORE AS NEEDED

JUICE OF ½ LEMON

1 RED ONION, SLICED THIN

1 LB. TOMATOES, SLICED

FRESH BASIL LEAVES, FOR GARNISH

FRESH PARSLEY, FINELY CHOPPED, FOR GARNISH

DIRECTIONS

1. Preheat the oven to 425°F. Place the chicken breasts in a bowl, season with salt and pepper, and then add the oregano, thyme, paprika, garlic, olive oil, and lemon juice. Stir until the chicken is evenly coated and set it aside.

2. Coat the bottom of a baking dish with olive oil and then distribute the red onion over it. Place the chicken breasts on top, arrange the tomato slices on top, and cover the baking dish with foil.

3. Place in the oven and roast for 10 minutes. Remove the foil and bake for another 5 to 7 minutes, until the chicken is cooked through. Remove from the oven and let rest for 10 minutes before garnishing with the basil and parsley.

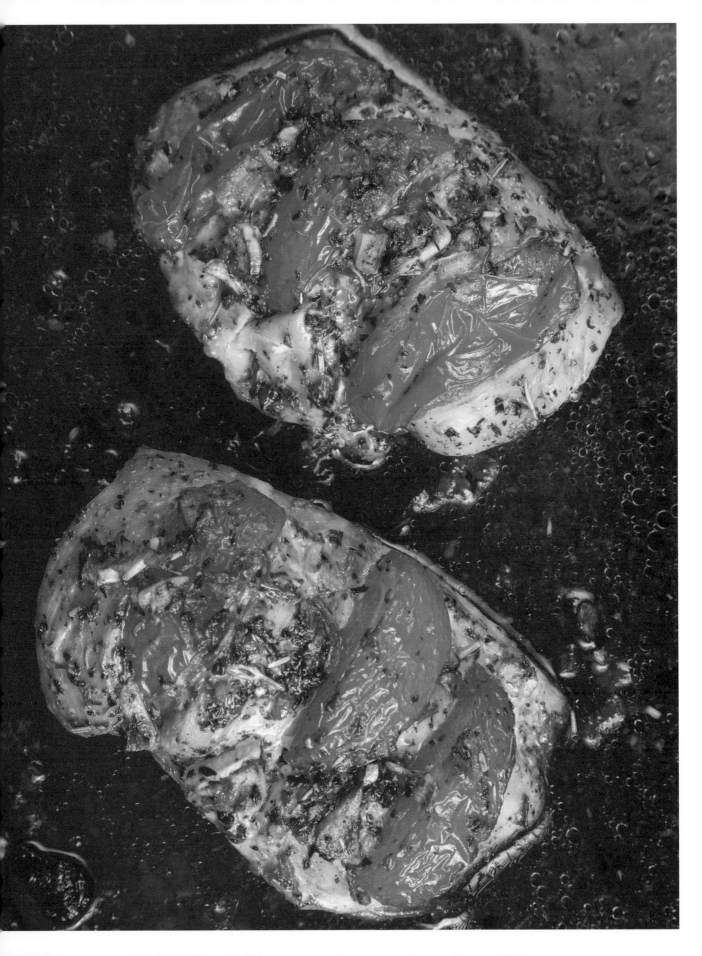

Chicken Souvlaki

INGREDIENTS

10 GARLIC CLOVES, CRUSHED

4 SPRIGS OF FRESH OREGANO

1 SPRIG OF FRESH ROSEMARY

1 TEASPOON PAPRIKA

1 TEASPOON KOSHER SALT

1 TEASPOON BLACK PEPPER

¼ CUP OLIVE OIL, PLUS MORE
AS NEEDED

¼ CUP DRY WHITE WINE

2 TABLESPOONS FRESH
LEMON JUICE

2½ LBS. BONELESS, SKINLESS
CHICKEN BREASTS, CHOPPED

2 BAY LEAVES

PITA BREAD (SEE PAGE 31),
WARMED, FOR SERVING

TZATZIKI (SEE PAGE 43),
FOR SERVING

2 TOMATOES, SLICED,
FOR SERVING

½ ONION, SLICED, FOR SERVING

2 CUCUMBERS, SLICED,
FOR SERVING

DIRECTIONS

1. Place the garlic, oregano, rosemary, paprika, salt, pepper, olive oil, wine, and lemon juice in a food processor and blitz to combine. Place the chicken and bay leaves in a bowl or a large resealable bag, pour the marinade over the chicken, and stir so that it gets evenly coated. Refrigerate for 2 hours, stirring or shaking occasionally.

2. Remove the chicken from the refrigerator, thread the pieces onto skewers, and allow them to come to room temperature. Prepare a gas or charcoal grill for medium-high heat (about 450°F).

3. Place the skewers on the grill and cook, turning frequently, until the chicken is cooked through, 6 to 8 minutes. Remove the skewers from the grill and let them rest briefly before serving alongside the pita, Tzatziki, tomatoes, onion, and cucumbers.

Chicken Shawarma

INGREDIENTS

2 LBS. BONELESS, SKINLESS
CHICKEN THIGHS

6 TABLESPOONS OLIVE OIL

3 TABLESPOONS RED
WINE VINEGAR

JUICE OF 2 LEMONS

2 TEASPOONS CINNAMON

2 TABLESPOONS CORIANDER

1 TABLESPOON BLACK PEPPER

1 TEASPOON CARDAMOM

1 TEASPOON GROUND CLOVES

½ TEASPOON MACE

PINCH OF GRATED FRESH NUTMEG

1 TABLESPOON GARLIC POWDER

2 YELLOW ONIONS, SLICED INTO
THIN HALF-MOONS

SALT, TO TASTE

1 TEASPOON SUMAC POWDER

1 CUP PLAIN GREEK YOGURT,
FOR SERVING

PITA BREAD (SEE PAGE 31),
FOR SERVING

2 PERSIAN CUCUMBERS, DICED,
FOR SERVING

2 PLUM TOMATOES, SLICED,
FOR SERVING

½ CUP FRESH MINT LEAVES, TORN,
FOR SERVING

DIRECTIONS

1. Place the chicken in a large mixing bowl. Add the olive oil, vinegar, lemon juice, cinnamon, coriander, pepper, cardamom, cloves, mace, nutmeg, and garlic powder and stir to combine. Place in the refrigerator and let it marinate for 1 hour. If time allows, let the chicken marinate overnight.

2. Place the sliced onions in a baking dish and cover with water. Add a pinch of salt and several ice cubes. Place in the refrigerator for 30 minutes.

3. Preheat your gas or charcoal grill to medium-high heat (450°F). Remove the meat from the refrigerator and let it come to room temperature. Drain the onions, squeeze to remove any excess water, and place them in a bowl. Add the sumac powder and toss to coat. Set them aside.

4. Place the chicken on the grill and cook, while turning, until it is browned all over and cooked through, 8 to 10 minutes. Remove from the grill and let rest for 10 minutes.

5. Chop the chicken into bite-sized pieces. Place a dollop of yogurt on a pita and top with some of the chicken, onions, cucumbers, tomatoes, and mint leaves.

Chicken Thighs with Tabbouleh

YIELD: **4 SERVINGS**

ACTIVE TIME: **15 MINUTES**

TOTAL TIME: **35 MINUTES**

INGREDIENTS

2 TABLESPOONS OLIVE OIL

4 BONE-IN, SKIN-ON CHICKEN THIGHS

SALT AND PEPPER, TO TASTE

2 TEASPOONS PAPRIKA

2 TEASPOONS CUMIN

2 TEASPOONS GROUND FENNEL

1 CUP CHERRY TOMATOES

2 GARLIC CLOVES, CRUSHED

1 SHALLOT, SLICED

½ CUP WHITE WINE

TABBOULEH (SEE PAGE 89)

DIRECTIONS

1. Preheat the oven to 450°F. Place the olive oil in a large cast-iron skillet and warm over medium-high heat. Season the chicken thighs with salt, pepper, paprika, cumin, and ground fennel. When the oil starts to shimmer, place the thighs in the pan, skin side down, and sear until browned, about 4 minutes. Turn the thighs over and place the pan in the oven. Roast until the internal temperature of each thigh is 165°F, about 16 minutes. Halfway through, add the tomatoes, garlic, and shallot to the pan.

2. When chicken is fully cooked, remove the pan from the oven and transfer it to a plate. Leave the vegetables in the pan, add the white wine, and place over high heat. Cook for 1 minute while shaking the pan. Transfer the contents of the pan to the blender, puree until smooth, and season to taste.

3. To serve, place some of the Tabbouleh on each plate. Top each portion with a chicken thigh and spoon some of the puree over the top.

Roasted Chicken with Roasted Roots & Brassicas

YIELD: **4 SERVINGS**

ACTIVE TIME: **30 MINUTES**

TOTAL TIME: **24 HOURS**

INGREDIENTS

1½ GALLONS CHICKEN BRINE
(SEE SIDEBAR)

5-LB. WHOLE CHICKEN

SALT AND PEPPER, TO TASTE

1 TABLESPOON FINELY CHOPPED
FRESH THYME

1 SWEET POTATO, PEELED
AND CHOPPED

1 CUP CHOPPED CELERY ROOT

2 CARROTS, PEELED AND CHOPPED

1 PARSNIP, TRIMMED
AND CHOPPED

2 CUPS BROCCOLI FLORETS

2 CUPS CAULIFLOWER FLORETS

2 TABLESPOONS OLIVE OIL

DIRECTIONS

1. Place the brine in a large stockpot, add the chicken, and place it in the refrigerator overnight. If needed, weigh the chicken down—plates are good for this—so it is submerged in the brine.

2. Remove the chicken from the brine and discard the brine. Place the chicken on a wire rack resting in a baking sheet and pat as dry as possible. Let sit at room temperature for 1 hour.

3. Preheat the oven to 450°F. Place the chicken in a baking dish, season lightly with salt and pepper, and sprinkle the thyme leaves on top. Place in the oven and roast until the juices run clear and the internal temperature in the thick part of a thigh is 160°F, about 35 minutes. Remove, transfer to a wire rack, and let it rest. Leave the oven on.

4. While the chicken is resting, place the remaining ingredients in a mixing bowl, season with salt and pepper, and toss to evenly coat. Place on a parchment-lined baking sheet and roast until tender, about 25 minutes. Remove, carve the chicken, and serve alongside the roasted vegetable medley.

CHICKEN BRINE

Place ¾ cup kosher salt, 6 tablespoons sugar, 6 cups room-temperature water, 1½ teaspoons whole black peppercorns, 5 crushed garlic cloves, 3 sprigs of fresh thyme, and 1 bay leaf in a large saucepan and bring the mixture to a boil, stirring to dissolve the sugar and salt. When these are dissolved, remove the pan from heat, transfer the mixture to a stockpot, and add 12 cups ice water and 4 cups ice. Let cool to room temperature before adding the chicken.

Kefta with Chickpea Salad

INGREDIENTS

1½ LBS. GROUND LAMB

½ LB. GROUND BEEF

½ WHITE ONION, MINCED

2 GARLIC CLOVES, ROASTED
AND MASHED

ZEST OF 1 LEMON

1 CUP FRESH PARSLEY, FINELY
CHOPPED

2 TABLESPOONS FINELY CHOPPED
FRESH MINT

1 TEASPOON CINNAMON

2 TABLESPOONS CUMIN

1 TABLESPOON PAPRIKA

1 TEASPOON CORIANDER

SALT AND PEPPER, TO TASTE

¼ CUP OLIVE OIL

CHICKPEA SALAD (SEE PAGE 61),
FOR SERVING

DIRECTIONS

1. Place all of the ingredients, except for the olive oil and the Chickpea Salad, in a mixing bowl and stir until well combined. Place a small bit of the mixture in a skillet and cook over medium heat until cooked through. Taste and adjust the seasoning in the remaining mixture as necessary. Working with wet hands, form the mixture into 18 ovals and thread them between six skewers.

2. Place the olive oil in a Dutch oven and warm over medium-high heat. Working in batches, add three skewers to the pot and sear the kefta until browned all over and nearly cooked through. Transfer the browned kefta to a paper towel–lined plate to drain.

3. When all of the kefta has been browned, return all of the skewers to the pot, cover it, and remove from heat. Let stand for 10 minutes so the kefta get cooked through.

4. When the kefta are cooked through, remove them from the skewers. Divide the salad between the serving plates, top each portion with the kefta, and serve.

YIELD: **6 SERVINGS**

ACTIVE TIME: **40 MINUTES**

TOTAL TIME: **2 HOURS AND 15 MINUTES**

Paella

INGREDIENTS

2 TABLESPOONS OLIVE OIL

2 LBS. HADDOCK FILLETS, CUBED

24 SHRIMP, SHELLED AND
DEVEINED

½ LB. SPANISH CHORIZO, SLICED

½ LARGE WHITE ONION, CHOPPED

1 BELL PEPPER, STEMMED, SEEDS
AND RIBS REMOVED, AND MINCED

4 GARLIC CLOVES, MINCED

SALT AND PEPPER, TO TASTE

1 CUP CHOPPED PLUM TOMATOES

3 CUPS MEDIUM-GRAIN RICE

6 CUPS SEAFOOD STOCK
(SEE PAGE 118)

½ CUP FRESH PARSLEY, CHOPPED

1 TEASPOON SAFFRON

1 TABLESPOON PIMENTON
(SPANISH PAPRIKA)

24 PEI MUSSELS, RINSED WELL
AND DEBEARDED

1 CUP PEAS

DIRECTIONS

1. Preheat the oven to 450°F. Warm a Dutch oven over
    medium-high heat and add the olive oil. When the oil starts
    to shimmer, place the haddock in the pan and cook for 2
    minutes on each side, until it is opaque throughout. Remove
    the haddock from the pan, add the shrimp, and cook for
    about 1 minute per side, so that it is cooked approximately
    three-quarters of the away through. Remove the shrimp from
    the pan and set it aside.

2. Place the chorizo, onion, bell pepper, and half of the garlic
    in the skillet and cook until the onion is slightly caramelized,
    about 10 minutes. Season with salt and pepper and add the
    tomatoes, rice, stock, the remaining garlic, parsley, saffron,
    and pimenton. Cook for 10 minutes, while stirring often.

3. Reduce heat to medium-low, cover the Dutch oven, and cook
    for 10 minutes.

4. Uncover the pot and add the haddock, shrimp, mussels,
    and peas. Cover the pot, place it in the oven, and cook until
    the majority of the mussels have opened and the rice is
    tender, about 12 minutes. Discard any mussels that have not
    opened. If the rice is still a bit crunchy, remove the haddock,
    mussels, and shrimp, set them aside, return pan to the
    oven, and cook until the rice is tender.

Chicken Legs with Potatoes & Fennel

INGREDIENTS

⅓ CUP OLIVE OIL, PLUS
2 TABLESPOONS

6 SKIN-ON CHICKEN LEGS

1 TABLESPOON KOSHER SALT,
PLUS MORE TO TASTE

1 TABLESPOON BLACK PEPPER,
PLUS MORE TO TASTE

5 SHALLOTS, CHOPPED

3 GARLIC CLOVES, MINCED

2 RED POTATOES, CHOPPED

4 YUKON GOLD POTATOES,
CHOPPED

3 FENNEL BULBS, TRIMMED,
CHOPPED, FRONDS RESERVED
FOR GARNISH

1 TEASPOON CELERY SEEDS

1 TEASPOON FENNEL SEEDS

½ CUP SUN-DRIED TOMATOES IN
OLIVE OIL, DRAINED

1 CUP CHARDONNAY

6 TABLESPOONS UNSALTED BUTTER

DIRECTIONS

1. Place a Dutch oven over medium-high heat and add the ⅓ cup of olive oil. Rub the chicken legs with the remaining oil and season with the salt and pepper. When the oil starts to shimmer, add half of the chicken legs to the pot, skin side down, and cook until the skin is golden brown and crusted, about 5 minutes. Remove, set aside, and repeat with the remaining chicken legs.

2. Preheat the oven to 400°F. Add the shallots and garlic to the Dutch oven and use a wooden spoon to scrape all of the browned bits from the bottom. Sauté until the shallots are translucent, about 3 minutes. Raise the heat to high and add the remaining ingredients, except for the wine and the butter. Cook, while stirring occasionally, for about 15 minutes.

3. Add the wine and the butter, stir, and then return the chicken to the pot, skin side up. Reduce the heat to medium-low, cover, and cook until the potatoes are tender and the chicken is 155°F in the center, about 30 minutes. Remove the lid, transfer the Dutch oven to the oven, and cook until the chicken is 165°F in the center. Garnish with the fennel fronds and serve.

Slow Cooker Cacciatore

INGREDIENTS

6 BONELESS, SKINLESS
CHICKEN THIGHS

1 (28 OZ.) CAN OF SAN MARZANO
TOMATOES, DRAINED

1 (28 OZ.) CAN OF DICED
TOMATOES, DRAINED

⅔ CUP DRY RED WINE

4 SHALLOTS, CHOPPED

3 GARLIC CLOVES, MINCED

1 GREEN BELL PEPPER,
STEMMED, SEEDS AND RIBS
REMOVED, AND CHOPPED

1 YELLOW BELL PEPPER, STEMMED,
SEEDED, AND DICED

1 CUP BUTTON MUSHROOMS,
CHOPPED

1½ TABLESPOONS DRIED OREGANO

1 TABLESPOON GARLIC POWDER

1 TABLESPOON SUGAR

2 TABLESPOONS KOSHER SALT,
PLUS MORE TO TASTE

½ TEASPOON RED PEPPER FLAKES

BLACK PEPPER, TO TASTE

PARMESAN CHEESE, GRATED,
FOR GARNISH

FRESH PARSLEY, FINELY CHOPPED,
FOR GARNISH

DIRECTIONS

1. Place all of the ingredients, save the Parmesan and parsley, in a slow cooker and cook on low until the chicken is very tender, about 5½ hours. The cooking time may vary depending on your slow cooker, so be sure to check after about 4½ hours to avoid overcooking.

2. To serve, top each portion with a generous amount of Parmesan cheese and parsley.

YIELD: **4 SERVINGS**

ACTIVE TIME: **20 MINUTES**

TOTAL TIME: **30 MINUTES**

Spinach & Feta Frittata

INGREDIENTS

6 EGGS

2 TABLESPOONS UNSALTED BUTTER

¼ CUP CHOPPED RED ONION

1 GARLIC CLOVE, MINCED

2 CUPS SPINACH, COARSE STEMS
REMOVED, CHOPPED

½ CUP CRUMBLED FETA CHEESE

SALT AND PEPPER, TO TASTE

DIRECTIONS

1. Set the oven's broiler to low. Place the eggs in a small bowl
   and beat until scrambled.

2. Warm a small cast-iron skillet over medium-high heat. Melt
   the butter in the skillet and add the onion and garlic. Sauté
   until the onion is translucent, about 3 minutes.

3. Add the spinach and cook, stirring continuously, until the
   leaves wilt. Sprinkle the feta over the mixture.

4. Pour the eggs into the skillet and shake the pan to evenly
   distribute them. Season with salt and pepper, cover the
   skillet, and cook until the eggs are set, about 10 minutes.

5. Place the skillet under the broiler and toast the top for about
   2 minutes. Remove and let stand for a couple of minutes.
   Season with salt and pepper before serving.

YIELD: **4 SERVINGS**

ACTIVE TIME: **20 MINUTES**

TOTAL TIME: **30 MINUTES**

Green Shakshuka

INGREDIENTS

1 TABLESPOON OLIVE OIL

1 ONION, CHOPPED

2 GARLIC CLOVES, MINCED

½ LB. TOMATILLOS, HUSKED, RINSED, AND CHOPPED

1 (12 OZ.) PACKAGE OF FROZEN SPINACH

1 TEASPOON CORIANDER

¼ CUP WATER

SALT AND PEPPER, TO TASTE

4 EGGS

TABASCO, FOR SERVING (OPTIONAL)

DIRECTIONS

1. Place the oil in a large skillet and warm it over medium-high. When the oil starts to shimmer, add the onion and sauté until just starting to soften, about 5 minutes. Add the garlic and cook until fragrant, about 1 minute. Add the tomatillos and cook until they have collapsed, about 5 minutes.

2. Add the spinach, coriander, and water and cook, breaking up the spinach with a fork, until the spinach is completely defrosted and blended with the tomatillos. Season with salt and pepper.

3. Evenly spread the mixture in the pan and then make four indentations in it. Crack an egg into each indentation. Reduce the heat to medium, cover the pan, and cook until the whites of the eggs are set, 3 to 5 minutes. Serve with Tabasco, if desired.

YIELD: **4 SERVINGS**

ACTIVE TIME: **10 MINUTES**

TOTAL TIME: **24 HOURS**

Ful Medames

INGREDIENTS

2 CUPS DRIED FAVA BEANS, SOAKED
OVERNIGHT AND DRAINED

4 GARLIC CLOVES, CHOPPED

¼ CUP OLIVE OIL, PLUS MORE
TO TASTE

JUICE OF 2 LEMONS

SALT AND PEPPER, TO TASTE

1 LARGE PINCH OF RED
PEPPER FLAKES

1 TEASPOON CUMIN

2 HARD-BOILED EGGS, EACH
CUT INTO 6 PIECES

2 TABLESPOONS FINELY
CHOPPED FRESH PARSLEY
OR MINT, FOR GARNISH

FETA CHEESE, CRUMBLED,
FOR SERVING (OPTIONAL)

BLACK OLIVES, FOR SERVING
(OPTIONAL)

DIRECTIONS

1. Place the beans in a Dutch oven, cover by ½ inch with water, and bring to a boil. Reduce the heat and simmer until tender, about 40 minutes. When the beans have about 10 minutes left to cook, stir in the garlic.

2. Drain, transfer the beans and garlic to a bowl, and add the olive oil, lemon juice, salt, pepper, red pepper flakes, and cumin. Lightly mash the beans with a fork and stir to combine.

3. Drizzle olive oil over the top of the mixture, transfer it to a platter, and place the pieces of hard-boiled egg on top. Garnish with parsley or mint and, if desired, serve with the feta cheese and black olives.

Stuffed Tomatoes

INGREDIENTS

6 LARGE TOMATOES

SALT AND PEPPER, TO TASTE

1 TABLESPOON OLIVE OIL

1 RED ONION, CHOPPED

4 GARLIC CLOVES, MINCED

½ GREEN BELL PEPPER, STEMMED, SEEDS AND RIBS REMOVED, AND CHOPPED

½ LB. GROUND TURKEY

1 TEASPOON CUMIN

1 TEASPOON FINELY CHOPPED FRESH OREGANO

½ TEASPOON ALLSPICE

½ TEASPOON GRATED FRESH NUTMEG

2 TEASPOONS RED PEPPER FLAKES

½ CUP COOKED LONG-GRAIN RICE

¼ CUP FINELY CHOPPED FRESH PARSLEY

¼ CUP FINELY CHOPPED FRESH MINT

DIRECTIONS

1. Cut off the tops of the tomatoes and use a spoon to scoop out the insides. Sprinkle salt into the cavities and turn the tomatoes upside down on a paper towel–lined plate. Let stand for about 30 minutes.

2. Place the olive oil in a 12-inch cast-iron skillet and warm it over medium-high heat. When the oil starts to shimmer, add the onion, garlic, and bell pepper and sauté until the onion is translucent, about 3 minutes. Add the turkey, cumin, oregano, allspice, and nutmeg, season with salt and pepper, and cook, breaking the turkey up with a fork, until it is browned, about 8 minutes.

3. Set the oven's broiler to high. Transfer the mixture to a mixing bowl, add the red pepper flakes, rice, parsley, and mint, and stir to combine. Fill the tomatoes' cavities with the mixture, wipe out the skillet, and arrange the tomatoes in the pan.

4. Place the stuffed tomatoes under the broiler and cook until the tops start to blister, about 5 minutes. Remove from the oven and serve immediately.

Skillet Salmon

INGREDIENTS

3 LBS. SALMON STEAKS, BONED

SALT AND PEPPER, TO TASTE

1 TEASPOON PAPRIKA

2 TABLESPOONS FINELY CHOPPED FRESH OREGANO

2 TABLESPOONS OLIVE OIL

ZEST AND JUICE OF 1½ LEMONS

3 GARLIC CLOVES, CRUSHED

ARUGULA, FOR SERVING

DIRECTIONS

1. Season the salmon steaks with salt and pepper and sprinkle the paprika and oregano over them. Let them rest at room temperature for 15 minutes.

2. Warm a large cast-iron skillet over medium-low heat for 5 minutes. Add the olive oil and raise the heat to medium. When it starts to shimmer, add the salmon and cook until browned, about 5 minutes. Turn the salmon over, add the lemon juice and garlic, and cook, spooning the pan sauce over the salmon, until it is cooked through, about 4 minutes.

3. Remove the salmon from the pan and let rest for 10 minutes. To serve, place each salmon steak on a bed of arugula, sprinkle the lemon zest over each portion, and drizzle the pan sauce on top.

Honey Mustard Salmon

INGREDIENTS

1½ LBS. SALMON FILLETS, BONED

SALT, TO TASTE

2 TABLESPOONS WHOLE-GRAIN MUSTARD

1 TABLESPOON HONEY

1 TABLESPOON OLIVE OIL

2 GARLIC CLOVES, MINCED

½ TEASPOON SMOKED PAPRIKA

¼ TEASPOON BLACK PEPPER

LIME WEDGES, FOR SERVING

DIRECTIONS

1. Preheat the oven to 375°F. Season the salmon fillets with salt and let them rest at room temperature for 15 minutes.

2. Place all of the remaining ingredients, except for the lime wedges, in a mixing bowl and stir to combine. Place the salmon in a baking dish and brush the honey mustard mixture on the salmon. Cover the dish with foil, place it in the oven, and bake the salmon for 15 minutes.

3. Remove the foil and set the oven's broiler to high. Broil the salmon until the tops of the fillets are browned and crispy, 2 to 3 minutes. Remove from the oven and serve with the lime wedges.

Grilled Swordfish

INGREDIENTS

8 GARLIC CLOVES, CRUSHED

⅓ CUP OLIVE OIL

2 TABLESPOONS FRESH LEMON JUICE, PLUS MORE FOR GARNISH

1 TEASPOON CORIANDER

1 TEASPOON CUMIN

1 TEASPOON SWEET PAPRIKA

1 TEASPOON KOSHER SALT

½ TEASPOON BLACK PEPPER

2 LBS. SWORDFISH FILLETS

DIRECTIONS

1. Preheat a gas or charcoal grill to high heat (500°F). Place all of the ingredients, except for the swordfish, in a blender and puree until smooth. Place the swordfish in a baking dish, pour the puree over it, and let the swordfish marinate at room temperature for 15 minutes.

2. Place the swordfish on the grill and cook for 5 minutes. Turn the swordfish over, cook for 3 minutes, and transfer to a platter. Let the swordfish rest for 5 minutes, drizzle more lemon juice over the top, and serve.

Garlic & Basil Baked Cod

INGREDIENTS

2 LBS. COD FILLETS

SALT AND PEPPER, TO TASTE

2 TABLESPOONS FINELY CHOPPED
FRESH OREGANO

1 TEASPOON CORIANDER

1 TEASPOON PAPRIKA

10 GARLIC CLOVES, MINCED

15 BASIL LEAVES, SHREDDED

6 TABLESPOONS OLIVE OIL

2 TABLESPOONS FRESH
LEMON JUICE

2 SHALLOTS, SLICED

2 TOMATOES, SLICED

DIRECTIONS

1. Place the cod in a mixing bowl or a large resealable plastic bag and add the remaining ingredients, except for the shallots and tomatoes. Stir to combine, place the mixture in the refrigerator, and let the cod marinate for 1 hour, stirring or shaking occasionally.

2. Preheat the oven to 425°F, remove the cod from the refrigerator, and let it come to room temperature. Cover the bottom of a baking dish with the shallots, place the cod on top, and top with the tomatoes. Pour the marinade over the mixture, place it in the oven, and bake for about 20 minutes, until the fish is flaky. Remove from the oven and let it rest briefly before serving.

YIELD: **4 SERVINGS**

ACTIVE TIME: **15 MINUTES**

TOTAL TIME: **25 MINUTES**

Salmon Burgers

INGREDIENTS

1½ LBS. SALMON FILLETS, BONED AND CHOPPED

1 TABLESPOON DIJON MUSTARD

2 SCALLIONS, TRIMMED AND MINCED

2 TABLESPOONS FINELY CHOPPED FRESH PARSLEY

1 TEASPOON CORIANDER

1 TEASPOON SUMAC POWDER

½ TEASPOON PAPRIKA

⅓ CUP ITALIAN BREAD CRUMBS

1 EGG, BEATEN

SALT AND PEPPER, TO TASTE

2 TABLESPOONS OLIVE OIL

4 WHOLE WHEAT HAMBURGER BUNS, FOR SERVING (OPTIONAL)

5 OZ. ARUGULA, FOR SERVING (OPTIONAL)

DIRECTIONS

1. Place the pieces of salmon in a food processor and pulse until ground, making sure the salmon retains some texture. Place the salmon in a bowl and incorporate the remaining ingredients, except for the olive oil and those designated for serving.

2. Form the salmon mixture into four patties. Place the olive oil in a skillet and warm it over medium heat. Place the patties in the pan and cook until browned, about 5 minutes. Turn the patties over, cover the pan, and cook until browned on the other side and cooked all the way through, about 5 minutes.

3. Remove the patties from the pan and serve on hamburger buns or over arugula.

Baked Salmon with Cilantro-Garlic Sauce

YIELD: **4 SERVINGS**

ACTIVE TIME: **10 MINUTES**

TOTAL TIME: **25 MINUTES**

INGREDIENTS

2 LBS. SALMON FILLETS, BONED

SALT AND PEPPER, TO TASTE

6 GARLIC CLOVES

1 BUNCH OF FRESH
CILANTRO, CHOPPED

½ CUP OLIVE OIL, PLUS MORE
AS NEEDED

2 TABLESPOONS FRESH LIME JUICE

2 TOMATOES, SLICED

1 LIME, SLICED

DIRECTIONS

1. Preheat the oven to 425°F. Season the salmon with salt and pepper and let it rest at room temperature as the oven warms up.

2. Place the garlic, cilantro, olive oil, lime juice, and a pinch of salt in a food processor and blitz until pureed.

3. Oil a baking dish and place the salmon in it. Spoon the garlic-and-cilantro puree over the salmon and then top it with the slices of tomato and lime.

4. Place the salmon in the oven and bake until the interior of the salmon is about 125°F, about 8 minutes. Remove from the oven, cover the dish with aluminum foil, and let it rest for 8 minutes. Serve with any remaining puree on the side.

NOTE: The cooking time assumes that the salmon fillets are each about 1 inch thick. If they are thinner or thicker, adjust the cooking times accordingly.

YIELD: **4 SERVINGS**

ACTIVE TIME: **10 MINUTES**

TOTAL TIME: **20 MINUTES**

Garlic & Lime Calamari

INGREDIENTS

1½ LBS. CALAMARI, SLICED INTO RINGS

2 TABLESPOONS OLIVE OIL

1 TABLESPOON UNSALTED BUTTER

10 GARLIC CLOVES, CHOPPED

3 TABLESPOONS WHITE WINE

JUICE OF 1½ LIMES

SALT AND PEPPER, TO TASTE

PINCH OF CAYENNE PEPPER

3 TABLESPOONS FINELY CHOPPED FRESH DILL

DIRECTIONS

1. Pat the calamari dry and set it aside. Place the olive oil and butter in a large cast-iron skillet and warm over medium-high heat. When the butter starts to foam, add the garlic and sauté until fragrant, about 1 minute.

2. Add the calamari to the pan, cook for 2 minutes, and then stir in the wine and lime juice. Cook for another 30 seconds, until warmed through, and remove the pan from heat. Season with salt and pepper, stir in the cayenne and dill, and serve.

YIELD: **4 SERVINGS**

ACTIVE TIME: **20 MINUTES**

TOTAL TIME: **45 MINUTES**

Greek Meatballs

INGREDIENTS

3 TABLESPOONS OLIVE OIL

1 SMALL ONION, CHOPPED

3 GARLIC CLOVES, MINCED

1 LARGE EGG

2 TABLESPOONS WHOLE MILK

1 TABLESPOON FRESH
LEMON JUICE

½ CUP ITALIAN BREAD CRUMBS

3 TABLESPOONS FINELY CHOPPED
FRESH OREGANO

2 TABLESPOONS FINELY CHOPPED
FRESH PARSLEY

1 TABLESPOON FINELY CHOPPED
FRESH MINT

1¼ LBS. GROUND LAMB

SALT AND PEPPER, TO TASTE

TZATZIKI (SEE PAGE 43),
FOR SERVING

TABBOULEH (SEE PAGE 89),
FOR SERVING

PITA BREAD (SEE PAGE 31),
FOR SERVING

DIRECTIONS

1. Preheat the oven to 450°F and line a rimmed baking sheet with aluminum foil. Place the oil in a small skillet and warm it over medium-high heat. When the oil starts to shimmer, add the onion and garlic and sauté until the onion is translucent, about 3 minutes. Remove the pan from heat and set it aside.

2. Place the egg, milk, lemon juice, bread crumbs, oregano, parsley, and mint in a mixing bowl and stir until combined. Add the lamb and onion mixture, season with salt and pepper, and stir until thoroughly combined. Working with wet hands, form the mixture into 1½-inch meatballs, arrange them on the baking sheet, and spray the tops with cooking spray.

3. Place the meatballs in the oven and bake for 12 to 15 minutes, until cooked through. Remove the pan from the oven and serve with Tzatziki, Tabbouleh, and Pita Bread.

Mint & Feta Meatballs

YIELD: **4 SERVINGS**

ACTIVE TIME: **20 MINUTES**

TOTAL TIME: **35 MINUTES**

INGREDIENTS

2 TABLESPOONS OLIVE OIL

2 SHALLOTS, CHOPPED

3 GARLIC CLOVES, MINCED

1 LARGE EGG

2 TABLESPOONS WHOLE MILK

½ CUP ITALIAN BREAD CRUMBS

½ CUP CRUMBLED FETA CHEESE

3 TABLESPOONS FINELY CHOPPED
FRESH MINT

1 TABLESPOON CUMIN

1 TEASPOON LEMON ZEST

PINCH OF CINNAMON

PINCH OF ALLSPICE

1¼ LBS. GROUND CHICKEN

SALT AND PEPPER, TO TASTE

TZATZIKI (SEE PAGE 43),
FOR SERVING

DIRECTIONS

1. Preheat the oven to 450°F and line a rimmed baking sheet with aluminum foil. Place the oil in a small skillet and warm over medium-high heat. When the oil starts to shimmer, add the shallots and garlic and sauté until the shallots are translucent, about 3 minutes. Remove the pan from heat and set it aside.

2. Place the egg, milk, bread crumbs, feta, mint, cumin, lemon zest, cinnamon, and allspice in a mixing bowl and stir to combine. Add the chicken and shallot mixture, season with salt and pepper, and stir until thoroughly combined. Working with wet hands, form the mixture into 1½-inch meatballs, arrange them on the baking sheet, and spray the tops with cooking spray.

3. Place the meatballs in the oven and bake for 12 to 15 minutes, until cooked through. Remove the pan from the oven and serve with Tzatziki.

YIELD: **4 SERVINGS**

ACTIVE TIME: **20 MINUTES**

TOTAL TIME: **45 MINUTES**

Sicilian Meatballs

INGREDIENTS

2 TABLESPOONS OLIVE OIL

½ SMALL RED ONION, CHOPPED

2 GARLIC CLOVES, MINCED

1 LARGE EGG

2 TABLESPOONS WHOLE MILK

½ CUP ITALIAN BREAD CRUMBS

¼ CUP GRATED PARMESAN CHEESE

¼ CUP PINE NUTS, TOASTED

3 TABLESPOONS MINCED
DRIED CURRANTS

2 TABLESPOONS FINELY CHOPPED
FRESH OREGANO

2 TABLESPOONS FINELY CHOPPED
FRESH PARSLEY

¾ LB. GROUND PORK

½ LB. SWEET OR SPICY GROUND
ITALIAN SAUSAGE

SALT AND PEPPER, TO TASTE

2 CUPS ROMESCO SAUCE
(SEE PAGE 97)

DIRECTIONS

1. Preheat the broiler to high, position a rack so that the tops of the meatballs will be approximately 6 inches below the broiler, and line a rimmed baking sheet with aluminum foil.

2. Place the oil in a large skillet and warm over medium-high heat. When it starts to shimmer, add the onion and garlic and sauté until the onion is translucent, about 3 minutes. Remove the pan from heat and set it aside.

3. Place the egg, milk, bread crumbs, Parmesan, pine nuts, currants, oregano, and parsley in a mixing bowl and stir until combined. Add the pork, sausage, and onion mixture, season with salt and pepper, and stir until thoroughly combined. Working with wet hands, form the mixture into 1½-inch meatballs, arrange them on the baking sheet, and spray the tops with cooking spray.

4. Place the meatballs in the oven and broil until browned all over, turning them as they cook. Remove the meatballs from the oven and set them aside.

5. Place the sauce in the skillet and warm over medium heat. Add the meatballs to the sauce, reduce the heat to low, cover the pan, and simmer, turning the meatballs occasionally, until they are cooked through, about 15 minutes. Season with salt and pepper and serve.

YIELD: **4 SERVINGS**

ACTIVE TIME: **25 MINUTES**

TOTAL TIME: **50 MINUTES**

Greek Tuna Balls

INGREDIENTS

2 TABLESPOONS MAYONNAISE

1 LARGE EGG

½ CUP ITALIAN BREAD CRUMBS

¼ CUP GRATED PARMESAN CHEESE

3 (5 OZ.) CANS OF TUNA, DRAINED AND FLAKED

SALT AND PEPPER, TO TASTE

2 TABLESPOONS OLIVE OIL

1 SMALL RED ONION, CHOPPED

3 GARLIC CLOVES, MINCED

1 CELERY STALK, CHOPPED

1 (28 OZ.) CAN OF CRUSHED TOMATOES, WITH THEIR LIQUID

½ CUP DRY WHITE WINE

¾ CUP PITTED AND CHOPPED KALAMATA OLIVES

¼ CUP CAPERS, DRAINED AND RINSED

¼ CUP CHOPPED FRESH PARSLEY

3 TABLESPOONS FINELY CHOPPED FRESH OREGANO

1 BAY LEAF

DIRECTIONS

1. Preheat the oven to 425°F and line a rimmed baking sheet with aluminum foil. Place the mayonnaise, egg, bread crumbs, and cheese in a mixing bowl and stir to combine. Fold in the tuna and season with salt and pepper.

2. Working with wet hands, form the mixture into 1½-inch balls, arrange them on the baking sheet, and spray the tops with cooking spray.

3. Place in the oven and bake for 8 to 10 minutes, until lightly browned. Remove from the oven and set aside.

4. While the tuna balls are in the oven, place the oil in a skillet and warm over medium-high heat. When it starts to shimmer, add the onion, garlic, and celery and sauté until the onion is translucent, about 3 minutes. Stir in the tomatoes, wine, olives, capers, parsley, oregano, and bay leaf and bring the sauce to a boil. Reduce the heat to medium and simmer the sauce for 15 minutes.

5. Add the tuna balls to the sauce and simmer for 10 minutes. Remove the bay leaf and discard it, season with salt and pepper, and serve immediately.

Falafel

INGREDIENTS

1 (14 OZ.) CAN OF CHICKPEAS

1 SMALL ONION, DICED

3 GARLIC CLOVES

¼ CUP ALL-PURPOSE FLOUR

2 TABLESPOONS FINELY CHOPPED FRESH PARSLEY

1 TABLESPOON FRESH LEMON JUICE

1 TABLESPOON CORIANDER

2 TEASPOONS CUMIN

1 TEASPOON BAKING SODA

SALT AND CAYENNE PEPPER, TO TASTE

VEGETABLE OIL, AS NEEDED

PITA BREAD (SEE PAGE 31), FOR SERVING

HUMMUS (SEE PAGE 48), FOR SERVING

DIRECTIONS

1. Drain the chickpeas and place them in a food processor. Add the onion, garlic, flour, parsley, lemon juice, coriander, cumin, baking soda, salt, and cayenne and blitz until the mixture is a smooth paste, scraping the work bowl as necessary.

2. Form the mixture into 1-inch balls, place them on a parchment-lined baking sheet, cover tightly with plastic wrap, and refrigerate for 20 minutes.

3. Add oil to a Dutch oven until it is approximately 2 inches deep and warm to 375°F over medium-high heat. Working in batches, add the falafel and fry until browned all over, about 3 minutes. Transfer the cooked falafel to a paper towel–lined plate to drain. When all of the falafel have been cooked, serve them with Pita Bread and Hummus.

METRIC CONVERSIONS

U.S. Measurement	Approximate Metric Liquid Measurement	Approximate Metric Dry Measurement
1 teaspoon	5 ml	5 g
1 tablespoon or ½ ounce	15 ml	14 g
1 ounce or ⅛ cup	30 ml	29 g
¼ cup or 2 ounces	60 ml	57 g
⅓ cup	80 ml	76 g
½ cup or 4 ounces	120 ml	113 g
⅔ cup	160 ml	151 g
¾ cup or 6 ounces	180 ml	170 g
1 cup or 8 ounces or ½ pint	240 ml	227 g
1½ cups or 12 ounces	350 ml	340 g
2 cups or 1 pint or 16 ounces	475 ml	454 g
3 cups or 1½ pints	700 ml	680 g
4 cups or 2 pints or 1 quart	950 ml	908 g

INDEX

ABOUT CIDER MILL PRESS
BOOK PUBLISHERS

Good ideas ripen with time. From seed to harvest, Cider Mill Press brings fine reading, information, and entertainment together between the covers of its creatively crafted books. Our Cider Mill bears fruit twice a year, publishing a new crop of titles each spring and fall.

"Where Good Books Are Ready for Press"
501 Nelson Place
Nashville, Tennessee 37214

cidermillpress.com